ENVIRONMENT FRIENDLY
HOME HINTS

General Editor
VERNA SIMPSON

EDITORIAL
General editor: Verna Simpson
Managing editor: Sheridan Carter
Sub-editor: Marian Broderick
Editorial co-ordinator: Margaret Kelly

DESIGN AND PRODUCTION
Monica Kessler-Tay
Chris Hatcher

ILLUSTRATIONS
Greg Gaul and Beth Norling

PUBLISHER
Philippa Sandall

Family Circle is a registered trademark ® of IPC
Magazines Limited.
Published by J. B. Fairfax Press by arrangement
with IPC Magazines Limited.

ENVIRONMENT FRIENDLY HOME HINTS
Includes Index
ISBN`1 86343 004 0

Formatted by J.B. Fairfax Press Pty Ltd
Output by Adtype, Sydney
Printed by Toppan Printing Co, Hong Kong

Distributed by J.B.Fairfax Press Pty Ltd
9 Trinity Centre, Park Farm Estate
Wellingborough Northants
Ph: (0933) 402330 Fax: (0933) 402234

ACKNOWLEDGEMENTS
The Publishers and the General editor would like to
thank Friends of the Earth, Australian Conservation
Foundation, Ecology International, Greenpeace,
The Total Environment Centre and the
Conservation Council of Victoria. The staff of all
these organisations have been enormously helpful
and all have opened their libraries. Special thanks
to Michael Kennedy for his valuable advice on
specialist areas, and to Teddi Purcell for her
relentless research.

All care has been taken to ensure the accuracy of
the information in this book but no responsibility
is accepted for any errors or omissions. The
publishers also wish to advise that herbs can be
quite potent and it is always best to consult a
qualified medical practitioner or professional
alternative practitioner before starting treatment
for a serious illness.

COVER: Jon Waddy (photography), Frank Pithers
(design), Sally Hirst (styling). Cover props supplied
courtesy Barbara's House and Garden.

CONTENTS

MEASURING UP

Metric Measuring Cups

1/4 cup	60 mL	2 fl.oz
1/3 cup	80 mL	2 1/2 fl.oz
1/2 cup	125 mL	4 fl.oz
1 cup	250 mL	8 fl.oz

Metric Measuring Spoons

1/4 teaspoon	1.25 mL
1/2 teaspoon	2.5 mL

MEASURING LIQUIDS

Metric	Imperial	Cup
60 mL	2 fl.oz	1/4 cup
125 mL	4 fl.oz	1/2 cup
170 mL	5 1/2 fl.oz	2/3 cup
250 mL	8 fl.oz	1 cup
500 mL	16 fl.oz	2 cups
600 mL	1 pint (20 fl.oz)	

MEASURING DRY INGREDIENTS

Metric	Imperial	Metric	Imperial
15 g	1/2 oz	350 g	11 oz
30 g	1 oz	375 g	12 oz
125 g	4 oz	500 g	16 oz (1lb)
185 g	6 oz	750 g	1 lb 8 oz
250 g	8 oz	1 kg	2 lb

INTRODUCTION

*The issues of pollution and the state of the environment
have become worldwide concerns. Every time we turn on TV
or read a newspaper we are treated to the latest
environmental debate. Issues like water pollution, the
Greenhouse Effect, ozone depletion and acid rain are
discussed over dinner tables in every corner of the globe.
This new awareness brings hope for the future. We all need
to work together to keep our planet
clean and free of toxic wastes.
Out of sight is no longer out of mind!
When you dispose of rubbish in the bin, onto the tip
and down the drain, it becomes part of the environment, for
better or for worse. The more toxic wastes you create, the
worse the problem becomes.
You and your family can help turn the tide. When you shop,
look for products that don't harm nature or pose
a potential health hazard.
This book is full of practical ideas and environment friendly
guidelines, including countless remedies,
old and new. There are hints and tips on home ecology for
every part of your home, including hundreds of recipes for
non-toxic cleaners and toiletries, ways to save water and
energy, how to set up your own organic garden and
compost, and everything you need to know about
growing and using herbs.*

SHOP TALK

- ❖ **The consumer cycle**
- ❖ **Recycling**
- ❖ **Disposable products**
- ❖ **Our endangered world**
- ❖ **Sympathetic packaging**
- ❖ **Paper and tissue**
- ❖ **Stationery**
- ❖ **How to make your own paper**
- ❖ **Food glorious food**
- ❖ **Cleaning**
- ❖ **Clothing**
- ❖ **Household appliances**
- ❖ **Buying a car**

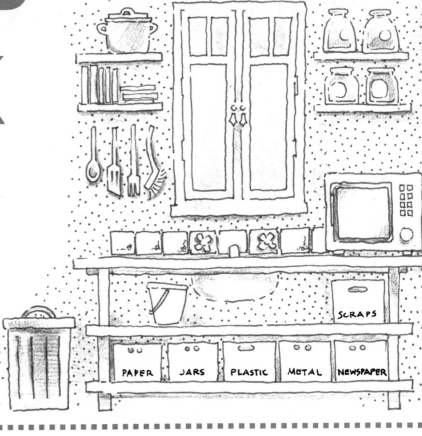

Shop 'til you drop? Shopping can be more than a day-to-day chore. For many of us it is a delight, and even an art form! For the environment, our shopping habits can be a killer.

❖ CONSUMER CYCLE ❖

It isn't easy at first to see the connection between shopping and the environment – that is, until you realise that so many of the things on your regular shopping list cause damage to the environment and pose a potential health hazard.

Products that end up in your home are a major cause of environmental problems worldwide. This section on shopping is packed with handy facts, hints and conservation tips to help you shop the healthy way for your family and the environment.

A good time to take a close look at your shopping habits is when you enter the consumer cycle at your local supermarket and shops. There are two main questions to ask yourself before you buy a product.

1 What is the product's lifespan? Its lifespan between purchase and disposal should be as long and useful as possible (excluding food items).

2 Is it environmentally friendly? How will you dispose of the product and/or its packaging? Can it be recycled? Is it biodegradable? Actively discourage manufacturers from producing and marketing goods that are environmentally harmful. Many of the items you buy one day will be garbage the next, so it's important to think ahead.

10 GOLDEN RULES

- ◆ **Buy local products**
- ◆ **Always take your own shopping bag**
- ◆ **Avoid 'disposable' items**
- ◆ **Buy organically grown fruit and vegetables**
- ◆ **Look for minimum packaging**
- ◆ **Avoid aerosol sprays**
- ◆ **Buy products in reusable or returnable containers**
- ◆ **Avoid plastic packaging**
- ◆ **Support shops that offer products friendly to the environment**
- ◆ **Buy both recycled and recyclable products**

IMPULSE BUYING

Think before you buy. Do you really need it? Any item purchased thoughtlessly and in a rush may be as bad for the environment as it is for your budget! How long before the item in question becomes garbage? Stop for a minute and think about it.

❖ START IN YOUR OWN BACKYARD ❖

You may well ask how you can make a difference to global environmental problems. The short answer is that you can make a big difference by starting in your own backyard.

◇ **Don't be afraid to speak out** in shops or at the supermarket. If the products you want are not available find out why, and ask for them to be stocked in future.

◇ **Always read the label.** Current laws require manufacturers to list the product's ingredients. Find out which food additives are harmful (see page 10).

◇ **Where is it made?** The label will also tell you where a product is made – support locally made products.

◇ **Is it harmful?** If it has been clearly proven that a product is harmful to the environment, don't buy it and make sure you tell the shopkeeper why. Ask for an alternative to be stocked. You don't have to be rude about it. If you keep asking politely for better products, it will pay off eventually.

◇ **Don't buy a second-rate substitute** if you can avoid it.

CAN YOU RECYCLE IT?

◇ **Buy recycled.** Buy products which have already been recycled or are made from and packaged in recyclable materials. Your local council will have all the necessary information about local recycling schemes, collection points and facilities, days, materials and so on.

◇ **Buy reusable products** or products in returnable containers – milk in glass bottles is still available from neighbourhood stores and many doorstep delivery services.

◇ **Glass, paper and card**, sorted metals and organic matter all have excellent recycling potential. Many local councils include glass bottles and jars in their recycling schemes. Ask for a bottle bank to be put in the car park at your local shopping centre or council waste depot.

◇ **Plastic is a problem.** It currently has very little recycling potential. Avoid where possible.

◇ **Products made from a mixture of different materials**, for example, plastic, metal and glass, so far have little recycling potential because of the complex and costly separation process involved.

> **FACT**
>
> Unlike materials such as paper, glass can be effectively recycled forever. Every tonne of crushed waste glass (or 'cullet') used saves the equivalent of 135 litres of oil and replaces 1.2 tonnes of raw materials.

LOCALLY MADE OR GROWN?

◇ **When purchasing** a product, take into account the distance the product has travelled to reach the shop shelf. When there's a choice between two similar items, opt for the one which has been made or grown locally.

◇ **The cost of transporting products** can't be measured in hard cash only. The packaging, processing and transportation stages cost enormously in energy resources and result in largescale waste and pollution. In the USA, the average food item travels 2100 km before being consumed.

◇ **Don't buy food out of season** if you can avoid it – this produce has usually been transported over vast distances to the point of sale. When you buy a mango in winter you can bet it has travelled half way round the world! If produce is locally grown and in season it will cost you less and you can be sure it's fresh.

❖ DISPOSABLE? Is it really? ❖

Over the last couple of decades we have become accustomed to buying throwaway 'convenience' products – less time equals less hassle. The gimmicky disposable tag has been splashed boldly across products as a big selling point.

Aggressive marketing and sales strategies have had a lot to do with the success of disposable products – their promotion has been so successful that everyone has come to rely on disposables. It's important that you help change this trend. What is convenient now may result in a longterm problem for the environment. Examine so-called disposable items carefully before buying them – how disposable are they really?

Next time you do your weekly shop, analyse what you buy. Isolate the items you'll use only once or twice before discarding and think about viable alternatives. Remember, although product packaging is designed to be easy to throw in the bin and forget, it's nothing of the sort.

COMMON DISPOSABLE ITEMS AND THEIR ALTERNATIVES	
DISPOSABLE?	**ALTERNATIVE**
Tea bags	Loose tea
Paper towels	Washable tea towels
Tissues	Handkerchiefs
Nappies	Cloth or join a nappy service
Aluminium baking trays	Baking tins
Plastic cling wrap	Reusable containers with lids
Plastic bin liners	Line kitchen bins with newspaper
Paper dust cloths ('j-cloths')	Washable dusters
Razors	Replaceable-blade razors
Pens	Refill only or a fountain pen
Paper napkins	Washable cloth napkins
Batteries	Rechargeable batteries
Paper kitchen towels	Washable dishcloths
Styrofoam cups	Washable cups
Paper plates	Washable plates
Plastic cutlery	Washable cutlery

◇ Every year more than 190,000 square kilometres of rainforest area is destroyed or grossly disturbed worldwide. This is a cause for concern because more than 50 per cent of the world's plant and animal species live in rainforests.

◇ Destruction of forest and other habitats is driving many species of plants and animals to extinction daily. This is tragic given that the genetic material being lost may contain the secrets for fighting many diseases and improving crops.

◇ Of an estimated 40,000 vertebrate species in the world 2,500 are currently threatened with extinction and at least 130 are already extinct due to the destruction of natural habitats.

◇ At-risk species include whales, birds, marsupials, sea turtles and dolphins.

Can you imagine a world without elephants, whales or seals? Don't buy products made from some part of an endangered species, like ivory from an elephant's tusk or snake skin. Unless steps are taken to protect different wildlife species, the result will eventually be dire. This doesn't just mean laying off the turtle soup! Be conservation-minded and selective whenever you buy products made from natural resources like rainforest timbers.

❖ SYMPATHETIC PACKAGING ❖

What is 'sympathetic' packaging? It is the minimum required to contain a product and keep it fresh. It should also be reusable or biodegradable and able to be recycled.

◇ **Don't buy over-packaged products** that are swaddled in layer upon layer of wrapping. Little or no packaging is best. Think of your budget as well as the waste – a large percentage of your weekly shopping bill is spent just on packaging.

◇ **Take your own shopping bag** or trolley with you when you go shopping. A sturdy canvas or string carry bag holds much more than a plastic one. Remember, plastics don't break down and can't be recycled, so any plastic bags you do have, try to reuse. Avoid plastic packaging.

◇ **Complain in writing** to the manufacturer if you think a product is outrageously over-packaged. If enough people respond in this way, the manufacturers will have to rethink the way their products are packaged. The power of the purse can be a very effective weapon.

FACT

Plastics that end up in the sea have been responsible for killing marine animals and birds. Plastics lodge in the intestines of whales, birds and fish choke on them, seals and dolphins get tangled up in them.

If your reply from the manufacturer is rude or unconcerned send a copy of both letters to your local newspaper for publication.

IT'S ONLY DRESSING!

◇ Avoid buying **products with individual packs inside.** This presentation is usually only 'dressing' and is often worth more than the product itself.

◇ **Cut down on canned food.** Fresh vegetables are better for you, tastier and just as easy to prepare. Why buy ham in a tin when you can buy it fresh from your delicatessen or butcher?

◇ **Buy soft drink in large bottles** rather than several small ones. Seek out reusable bottles, these are even better than recyclable. Glass milk bottles are refilled an average of 36 times, and can then be recycled when broken.

◇ **Buy fresh, not frozen.** Treats like apple pies and other pastries will be fresher, more tasty and better value for money from your local cake shop or bakery than frozen from the supermarket.

◇ **Cut down on takeaways.** Instead of a takeaway meal packaged up in throwaway containers, take the family out to eat. It may cost a little more, but will be enjoyed by all and won't create unnecessary waste.

◇ **Cut down on plastic bags.** Don't put your vegetables into plastic bags. Keep them loose or together until you need them. Don't forget to wash them before use.

◇ Avoid buying **prepackaged vegetables or fruit** on styrofoam trays with plastic wrap pulled over. These 'on special' packs are a presentation ploy and often conceal second-rate or rotten produce.

◇ **Buy in bulk** for your family every week. Phone the manufacturers and ask if bulk amounts are available and where you can purchase them. Healthfood shops and food co-operatives are an excellent source of bulk produce. Take your own containers and have them refilled.

Sample letter to manufacturer

Dear Managing Director

Re: Product packaging

Today I almost bought a packet of your XXXXXXX. I decided against it when I realised there were seven outer layers of packaging, made up of three different types of material: foil, plastic and cardboard.

I will not buy this product in future unless the packaging material can be recycled and is reduced to two layers. As it is, your excessive packaging relies on non-renewable resources and creates an unnecessary amount of instant garbage that is not disposable in an environmentally acceptable way.

I will also be recommending to my friends and neighbours that they don't buy your product. I have already asked my local suppliers not to stock it in future.

I sincerely hope that you will be reviewing your product packaging in the near future.

Yours sincerely

Jean Jones

USE BY
The USE BY date on a product indicates the date by which it must be consumed, for example, USE BY 11 March 1992. Packed meats, prepackaged dishes, dairy produce and most breads and cakes generally have a date stamp. Never buy outdated foodstuffs.

Lifecycle of a disposable Nappy

SUPER MARKET

❖ PAPER AND TISSUE ❖

Use paper wisely and participate in recycling schemes. Large quantities of trees, water and energy are used in the production of paper, and the dyes, bleaches and other chemicals required pollute the air and water. Help by being more thoughtful in your purchase, use and disposal of paper and paper products.

◇ Use **handkerchiefs** instead of tissues. Handkerchiefs are re-usable and don't cost forests of trees to produce. Try to cut down generally on tissues, paper towels and napkins. Change to recycled toilet paper – the colour may take a little getting used to but that is a small price to pay for more trees and cleaner air.

◇ **No junk mail.** Junk mail uses up massive quantities of paper. If you don't want to receive any, put a clear sign on your letter box that reads NO JUNK MAIL.

◇ **Please don't deliver.** If you don't read the free local newspaper, put a sign on your letterbox to stop delivery.

◇ **Extend its life.** Share newspapers, magazines and books with neighbours or give them to hospitals, charities and libraries.

◇ **Always recycle your paper.** Most local councils have regular collection days. Find out when they are and participate.

STATIONERY

◇ **Buy recycled paper** and maximise the use of your paper by writing on both sides and reusing envelopes.

◇ Avoid stationery gift items with **excessive packaging**. Pens are often packaged in a blister pack four times larger than the pen itself. Unpackaged stationery is usually cheaper.

◇ **Buy pens that take refills.** When your disposable pen runs dry, check that the ink has actually run out before you throw it away.

◇ **Make it last longer.** If a pen still has ink, immerse it in warm water for 15 minutes, or wrap in foil and place in a warm oven to encourage the ink to flow again.

◇ **Invest in a stylish fountain pen** that will last you for years.

❖ HOW TO MAKE YOUR OWN PAPER ❖

MATERIALS

☐ **scrap paper (not newspaper or thick glossy magazine paper)**
☐ **water**
☐ **an electric blender**
☐ **a mould, or 'deckle', to shape the paper (see below)**
☐ **starch (optional)**
☐ **kitchen wipes (or squares of calico larger than the deckle)**

To make the mould

Using smooth timber, make two identical shapes similar to a picture frame. Size of mould determines the size of the paper produced. The timber should be flat on the top and the bottom. Set one aside. Cover the bottom of the other with muslin or cheesecloth – be sure to pull it firmly across the mould and slightly down the sides. Staple or tack it in place securely.

Pulp

Tear up paper into pieces about 4 cm x 4 cm. Add quantity of paper with water to blender. Mix until thoroughly pulped. Pour pulp into oblong basin – not circular. Strongly coloured paper will tint the mixture and result in coloured paper. To make paper which is suitable for calligraphy, add a small quantity of powdered starch to pulp to stop the ink running (1 tablespoon per square basin).

To use mould

Place the open mould on top of covered mould so that the fabric forms a middle layer. Holding the two firmly together, slide them through the paper mixture, scooping up pulp into mould. Allow to drain on side of basin, take off top frame, flip pulp onto damp kitchen wipe laid across damp towel (called a 'couch').

Layer pulp with kitchen wipes or similar, until 6-7 layers have built up. Place layers onto floor, place bread board on top of layers, stand on top to squeeze excess water out. Take each layer of pulp/paper and place between layers of newspaper until dry. Peel away kitchen wipes and your paper will be ready to use.

❖ FOOD GLORIOUS FOOD ❖

When you have a busy schedule to keep up with there's not always time to stop and check the label on a can or make sure that the vegetables are super fresh. Slow down long enough to really look at what you're buying, especially if it means safeguarding your family's health.

ORGANICALLY GROWN?

When you buy organically grown fruit and vegetables you can be 100 per cent certain that they are pesticide-free. Organic farming avoids using any chemicals in the raising and harvesting of crops and uses energy more efficiently because all wastes are recycled.

Your local healthfood shop will be able to direct you to the nearest available retail source or food co-operative. Even better, why not experiment with your own smallscale organic garden and taste the difference? (See pages 56-75.)

FOOD ADDITIVES

Food additives are used in commercial food preparation to enhance a product's flavour, texture or colour and to extend its life. Salt and sugar are the most common additives and both should be used in moderation. Always read the label carefully and control your intake. If your diet centres around fresh, unprocessed foods, the less you need to worry about the effects of food additives.

Most food and drink product ranges offer a choice and there's usually at least one brand that is free of additives or preservatives – orange juice is a good example. If you browse along the supermarket shelves you'll notice a selection of 100 per cent natural products.

BUY IN MODERATION

What percentage of the food you buy each week is wasted? Make a record of the food you buy in a typical week, noting what gets eaten and how much is thrown out – you may be in for a shock! Try to plan your weekly menus and buy only what you need.

Don't fall into the trap of buying large amounts of perishable food just because it's on special. Although hard to resist, a

BREAK THE CODE

In most countries, the law requires a product's ingredients to be listed. To simplify this, international numeric codes have been devised and must be displayed on the label.

TARTRAZINE

A bright yellow coal-tar dye (known in the USA as FD&C Yellow No. 5, in the EEC as E102), found in many soft drinks and confectionery products. It has been known to cause a wide range of allergies and symptoms of intolerance, including hyperactivity, asthma, migraine and skin rashes.

FOOD ADDITIVES HYPERACTIVE CHILDREN SHOULD AVOID

E102	Tartrazine
E104	Quinoline yellow
E123	Amaranth
E124	Ponceau 4R
E127	Erythrosine
128	Red 2G
E132	Indigo carmine
133	Brilliant blue FCF
E150	Caramel
E151	Black PN
154	Brown FK
E110	Sunset Yellow FCF
E120	Cochineal
E122	Carmoisine
155	Brown HT
E210	Benzoic acid
E211	Sodium benzoate
E220	Sulphur dioxide
E250	Sodium nitrite
E251	Sodium Nitrate
E320	Butylated hydroxyanisole
E321	Butylated hydroxytoluene

DANGEROUS TO ASTHMATICS AND ASPIRIN-SENSITIVE PEOPLE

E212	Potassium benzoate
E213	Calcium benzoate
E214	Ethyl 4-hydroxybenzoate
E215	Ethyl 4-hydroxybenzoate, sodium salt
E216	Propyl 4-hydroxybenzoate
E218	Methyl 4-hydroxbenzoate
E219	Methyl 4-hydroxbenzoate, sodium salt
E221	Sodium sulphite
E222	Sodium bisulphite
E223	Sodium metabisulphite
E224	Potassium metabisulphite
E310	Propyl gallate
E311	Octyl gallate
E312	Dodecyl gallate
621	Sodium hydrogen L-glutamate
622	Potassium hydrogen L-glutamate
623	Calcium dihydrogen di-L-glutamate
627	Guanosine 5' (disodium phosphate)
635	Sodium 5' (ribonucleotide)

bargain can turn out to be a false economy if most of it ends up in the bin. On the other hand, if the large quantity of tomatoes you buy at your local fruit and vegetable market makes a year's supply of tomato relish – that's a real bargain!

JOIN A FOOD CO-OPERATIVE

Joining or even starting up a neighbourhood food co-operative is a great way to ensure you get fresh produce at the right price all year round. If there are about 20 people in the co-operative, each member will only have to go to the markets about three times a year.

A co-operative saves time, energy and money and provides an excellent basis for networking in your community.

FAST FOOD

The rise of fast-food chains has coincided with the boom industry in food prepared outside the home. But there is an added cost which many consumers are unaware of.

The worldwide problems created by clearing forests to make pasture for beef cattle are well documented. The burning of forests and natural digestive fermentation in cattle produce about 40 per cent of the methane rising in the tropics. Methane is a Greenhouse gas.

GREENHOUSE GASES

Carbon Dioxide from burning forests
Methane
Nitrous Oxide
Rainforest destroyed to make way for pasture
Nitrogen based fertiliser causes buildup of Nitrous Oxide
FAST

FOR YOUR INFORMATION

There are five major types of food additives:

1 Preservatives inhibit the growth of bacteria which would otherwise cause the food to rot or become poisonous.

2 Antioxidants prevent oils and fats from turning rancid, thereby extending the shelf lives of products containing these ingredients.

3 Cosmetic additives modify the taste, appearance and texture of food products.

4 Processing aids are used by the manufacturer to facilitate the processing of a product and/or its passage through packaging equipment, e.g. anti-foaming products or clarifying agents.

5 Nutrients such as vitamins, calcium and minerals.

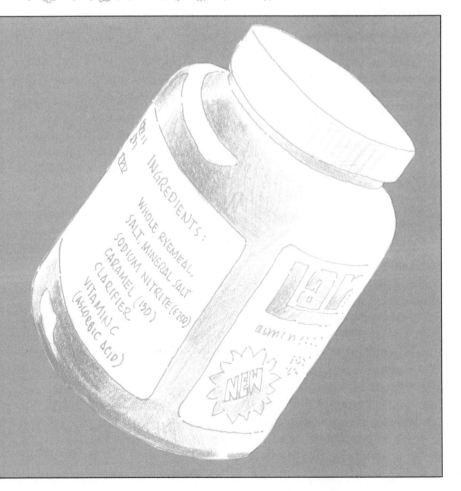

INGREDIENTS: WHOLE RYEMEAL, SALT, MINERAL SALT, SODIUM NITRITE (E250), CARAMEL (150), CLARIFIER, VITAMIN C (ASCORBIC ACID)

NEW

❖ KEEP IT CLEAN! ❖

'Cleanliness is next to Godliness', or so the saying goes. These days you can buy a different cleaning product for just about any surface or material in existence.

Many of the wonder cleaning products recommended for use in the home are poisonous to plants and animals, so when you pour them down the drain you pollute the water system and kill living organisms, and when you spray aerosols you are damaging the atmosphere.

There is really no substitute for good old-fashioned soap and a little elbow grease. Try to cut down on cleaners and be aware of their real effects. Buy or make natural cleaning products and use only moderate amounts. Read our section on Down-to-earth Home Hints (pages 16-29) for all the natural recipes you'll ever need to keep your home clean and friendly.

ALL ABOUT DETERGENTS
The first synthetic detergents were made in 1907. Before then, soaps were used to clean just about everything. The range of detergents has increased so dramatically that today there are as many cleaning agents as cleaning jobs.

Detergents are made from petrochemicals, a non-renewable resource, and many detergents are not readily biodegradable.

Following are some of the ingredients you will find in synthetic detergents.

◇ **Phosphates** are used to soften water. They also cause major problems in waterways by encouraging weed growth, which in turn robs aquatic life of oxygen. Lifeless streams and rivers are the end result. Phosphates have been banned in Switzerland and many States of the USA.

◇ **Surface active agents** reduce the surface tension of washing water, allowing fabric to be properly wet through.

◇ **Disinfectants** kill the bacteria which cause infection. Unfortunately they also kill the good bacteria needed to decompose sewage. Disinfectant use should be kept to a minimum.

◇ **Optical brighteners** make washed fabrics appear whiter or brighter by absorbing ultraviolet light and re-emitting blue light. This gives the appearance of whiteness but is not a guarantee of cleanliness.

◇ **Fillers** are inert additives which provide bulk and alkalinity.

◇ **Foam boosters** add suds but don't affect or enhance cleaning action.

◇ **Perfumes** add a cosmetic fresh smell to clothes (but don't be deceived, the smell is manufactured, not real).

◇ **Enzymes** attack protein and carbohydrate grime, soil and stains. They can also cause allergic reactions.

REMEMBER
There is no such thing as a completely clean home. We need many of the bacteria which live in the environment to protect us against other more harmful organisms. So, although cleanliness and hygiene are important, obsessive cleanliness is unnecessary.

One squirt will do. Most people use twice as much detergent as they need to.

Pure soap has been made for thousands of years and is still the best detergent going. Today the word 'detergent' is more commonly associated with synthetic rather than natural soap. Replace synthetic detergents with soap at every opportunity – soap is non-toxic, biodegradable and cheap.

◇ Detergents cause **domestic accidents** through poisoning more than any other household product. Young children are particularly at risk. Keep detergents in high places out of reach of small, exploring hands.

◇ **Read the ingredients list** on the packet.

ALL-PURPOSE CLEANER

Mix together 50 mL of cloudy ammonia, 50 mL of vinegar and 120 mL of bicarbonate of soda with 4 litres of hot water. Put the solution in a simple pump-action spray bottle or pour straight onto your cleaning cloth. Shake mixture well before use and avoid inhaling ammonia vapour.

◇ Avoid **phosphate detergents**. The phosphates in synthetic detergents pollute our water and endanger native flora and fauna. Phosphates are essential nutrients for plants but, like many other such substances, they can cause serious pollution if present in excessive quantities.

◇ Use **synthetic detergents** sparingly. You can reduce the recommended amount of most detergents by half without any noticeable difference to the end result.

◇ Dilute all **liquid cleaners** when you buy them by adding an equal amount of water.

◇ **Rinse dishes well.** If using a commercial dishwashing liquid, make sure you rinse dishes and cutlery well – detergents leave a residue which is more harmful to you than the grease you're trying to erase.

Household cleaning products are designed to disinfect, clean and deodorise your home until it smells like a pine forest or a field of roses! This fantasy disguises the more insidious effects of bleach, air fresheners and detergents. The bad, longterm effects of these substances will be minimised if you reduce the amount you buy each week.

If the manufacturers are to be believed, cleaning happens by magic and your kitchen or bathroom is instantly transformed by one of their wonder products! Don't be taken in by advertising gimmicks. Non-toxic cleaning is effective and cheap, and requires far fewer cleaning supplies.

WHAT TO BUY

There's no need to return to the days of washboards and housemaid's knee! All the ingredients you'll ever need for natural cleaners to keep your home fresh and clean are on our list.

☐ **Washing soda** is a natural water softener and grease cutter. Used in moderation, it is a good heavy-duty cleaner for floors and walls. Added to your wash, washing soda helps clean really dirty clothes.

☐ **Bicarbonate of soda** (baking soda) is infinitely useful around the home as a water softener, scouring powder, oven cleaner, stain remover, plaque buster, chrome polisher and facial cleanser. Look for the biggest pack you can buy.

☐ **Vinegar** is inexpensive and can be used for hundreds of household chores. Look for the largest containers.

☐ **Salt** is an abrasive but benign scouring powder. It is also mildly antiseptic. Buy in bulk and preferably not in a plastic container.

☐ **Lemon** essence can be added to your homemade cleaners for that lemon-fresh smell. Lemon juice is also an effective stain remover.

☐ **Essential oils** can be used to perfume homemade cleaners. Include olive oil or even vegetable oil as ingredients in homemade furniture and wood polishes.

☐ **Household soap or pure soap flakes** are all you need for many cleaning and washing tasks.

☐ **Ammonia** is good for oven cleaning and as an ingredient in a general all-purpose cleaner. Avoid inhaling ammonia vapour.

☐ **Borax**, a natural salt, is available through pharmacies and is a substitute for chlorine bleach. It can be used to increase the effectiveness of plain soap, to soften water, whiten clothes, control mould and prevent unpleasant odours.

☐ **Vanilla essence** can be used to eliminate unpleasant household smells.

☐ **Flour** is good for polishing chrome and other metals.

AVOID AEROSOL SPRAYS

The first living creature to die from an aerosol spray was a mosquito in 1942! Since then the aerosol industry has moved beyond pesticides into a wide variety of consumer products.

Scientific evidence has shown that certain aerosol propellants, known as chlorofluorocarbons (CFCs), are a contributing factor in the depletion of the ozone layer. Although fluorocarbons are being phased out worldwide, substitute propellants still damage the atmosphere.

Aerosol sprays are no more effective than the age-old methods of pouring, wiping or dusting. The billions of aerosol sprays produced annually waste vast amounts of steel, plastic, paper and energy resources. The spray valve alone on a can of aerosol has several separate plastic parts.

An aerosol can is never completely emptied and if the can has a faulty valve it has to be discarded. Clogged nozzles, common with spray starches and powders, can be wasteful and costly. Other liquid, solid or pump-spray products can be used to the last drop.

HAIRSPRAY
Although some hairsprays are now available in a non-aerosol spray can, the propellant gases used in most hairsprays are not the only reason to avoid them. They contain highly toxic plastic resin which is not only harmful to skin and eyes but can also cause a lung disease called thesaurosis. Although this disease can be treated, why not choose a non-toxic gel or a homemade hairspray instead?

TYPICAL AEROSOL FORMATIONS

PRODUCT CONCENTRATE	PROPELLANT (CFCs)	PRODUCT (ACTUAL)
Underarm deodorant		
Type A	45%	55%
Type B	90%	10%
Insect repellent	70%	30%
Oven cleaner		
Type A	25%	75%
Type B	10%	90%
Antiperspirant		
Type A	30%	70%
Type B	90%	10%
Feminine hygiene spray	95%	5%

❖ CLOTHING ❖

'Clothes maketh the man' or woman, and no clothes are quite so wonderful next to your skin as natural fibres like cotton, wool or silk.

◇ Avoid **man-made fibres** if you can – even those present in mixtures, for example, polycotton.

◇ Choose **leather shoes** over plastic.

◇ Don't buy **snake and crocodile skin shoes** or fur coats.

◇ Avoid **dry cleaning** as this cleaning process makes use of toxic chemicals which are bad for your clothes and the environment. Most fabrics don't require dry cleaning – manufacturers label almost everything 'Dry Clean Only' for their own protection.

◇ **Care for your fabrics.** All fabrics need to be well looked after if you want them to last. Some fabrics need extra special care, so always check the care label when buying them. If possible, buy machine-washable items particularly bed linen and children's clothes, and buy drip-dry clothes to save ironing.

◇ **Care labels.** All garments made must have a label on them with details of how to care for them in symbols and words. Care labels usually indicate whether a fabric is suitable for tumble drying, drip drying, line drying or drying flat.

PURE SOAP FLAKES
◇ Can be used in hot or cold water.
◇ Good for hand washing.
◇ Best for soft-water areas. In hard-water areas, add bicarbonate of soda as a water softener.
◇ Use for delicate woollens, articles which are not very dirty, or man-made fibres.

❖ HOUSEHOLD APPLIANCES ❖

When you're thinking about buying a new appliance, the first question to ask yourself is do you really need it? The market is flooded with gadgets that are expensive to buy and run.

◇ **Time-saving gadgets.** How many fantastic, time-saving gadgets do you have tucked away in cupboards that you haven't even looked in for years? Why not have a garage sale, give them to a charity or offer them to a friend in need?

◇ **Shop around.** Check the labels on different appliances for energy consumption levels . Buy an appliance low in energy use. Also ask about replacement parts and servicing – you want to get as many years use out of the appliance as possible. It is often easier to get replacement parts for a locally-made appliance.

◇ **Buy equipment that suits your needs.** If there are only two of you, buy a small fridge and washing machine. A large family will need more heavy-duty appliances that will last the distance over the years.

◇ **Choice matters.** Appliances with a range of settings are more versatile – for example, washing machines with a half-load option or a short cycle for the not-so-dirty wash.

◇ **Buy solar-powered equipment.** It is cheap, clean and effective, and doesn't deplete a non-renewable resource.

FRIDGES AND FREEZERS

◇ Make a note of the measurements of the unit and the space in the kitchen before you buy anything. Sizes range from small worktop fridges to huge free-standing ones. An average family of four is supposed to need about 242 litres (8.4 cu ft) of refrigeration. All fridges and freezers need ventilation for the motor.

◇ A combined fridge-freezer may be the answer to a space problem.

◇ Find one with the freezer at the bottom and the fridge at the top for greatest convenience.

◇ Choose a fridge or freezer with a door that opens in the right direction. Some models can have the door hinged on the right or the left, some are adjustable.

◇ Choose a fridge with suitable fittings (sometimes simple shelves are more convenient than egg racks and other compartments). Adjustable shelves can be very useful.

❖ BUYING A CAR ❖

When you buy a new car, the smaller, the better – and much easier to park too! Unless you need a powerful car to pull a caravan or accommodate a large family, look for a small, easy-to-park vehicle with low fuel consumption.

◇ Compare **engine efficiencies**. Similar-sized engines can vary in efficiency. Always check a car's likely fuel consumption.

◇ Avoid **energy-consuming extras**. Air conditioning increases fuel use by around 10 per cent and uses CFCs, one of the Greenhouse gases depleting the ozone layer. A manual car uses 10 per cent less fuel than an automatic.

Down-to-earth HOME HINTS

- ❖ **Your kitchen**
- ❖ **Your bathroom**
- ❖ **Your laundry**
- ❖ **General cleaning tips**
- ❖ **Air fresheners**
- ❖ **Pot pourri**
- ❖ **Household pests**
- ❖ **Just for you**

All household pollutants eventually make their way into the water, soil and atmosphere. Make a point of knowing what chemicals are present in your home – it could be a matter of life or death.

MOTHPROOFING
◇ Scatter dried orange peel through clothing in drawers.
◇ Place muslin bags, each containing 50 g of ground cloves, cinnamon, black pepper and orris root, among the clothes.
◇ Place lavender in gauze sachets between the layers and folds of clothing.

❖ HOME, SWEET HOME ❖

Home is the last place we associate with environmental pollution, even though we spend over half our time there, and stock a wide range of environmentally harmful chemicals. Our cupboards of chemicals contain detergents, air fresheners and deodorisers, solvents, stain removers, toiletries, disinfectants, insect repellents, insecticides, garden sprays and pesticides.

This section is packed with practical hints, tips and natural recipes for a chemical-free home. By using a small range of natural, inexpensive ingredients, you can make your own cleaning products to suit any job. Later, in the gardening section, we also present a whole range of natural alternatives to using chemical products in your garden.

Take a good look at the range and quantity of chemical products you stock. Do they display a list of ingredients? Are you familiar with the chemicals used and their longterm effects? Are they potentially dangerous? How will they affect the environment?

Always check the list of ingredients so that you know what the product contains. Look critically at the packaging and type of container. How disposable is it? Can it be recycled? Where cleanliness is concerned, a good standard of hygiene is vital, but obsessive cleanliness, especially by means of chemicals, is unnecessary.

10 GOLDEN RULES

◆ **Make or buy non-toxic cleaners**
◆ **Avoid pesticide use in the home**
◆ **Read labels carefully**
◆ **Use all cleaners moderately**
◆ **Keep your toiletries simple**
◆ **Avoid over-packaged cosmetics and cleaners**
◆ **Learn which additives are harmful and avoid them**
◆ **Choose biodegradable products**
◆ **Avoid aerosol cleaners**
◆ **Buy products that have not been tested on animals**

❖ YOUR KITCHEN ❖

Hygiene and daily cleaning are very important in your kitchen because of the grease and condensation caused by cooking.
While many chemicals are convenient to use for cleaning, there are pressing environmental reasons to use natural cleaning methods and non-toxic products.

◇ **Blocked drains:** Use a rubber plunger. Clean grease-blocked drains by soaking with washing soda and hot water, or pour a handful of bicarbonate of soda down the drain, followed by half a cup of vinegar. Replace the plug and close the drain. Let it sit for a while, then flush with water. Prevent drains blocking in the first place by not pouring grease down your sink.

◇ **Burnt pots:** Dissolve 2 teaspoons of bicarbonate of soda in water, bring to the boil and clean when cool. Alternatively, fill the pot with water, add a good handful of salt, bring to the boil and soak overnight. You can also use potato peelings instead of salt (soak overnight and then boil). Badly burnt pans can be cleaned by gently heating a little olive oil in them. Allow to stand for an hour, pour off the oil into a container (for later disposal) and clean in the usual way. Fill stained pots with water, add the peel and core of an apple and boil mixture to remove marks.

ESSENTIALS

Most cleaning requires simple solutions and good, old-fashioned elbow grease. Keep a stock of bicarbonate of soda, white vinegar, cloudy ammonia and pure soap. These can be combined to make a whole range of environment-friendly cleaners. To clean:

◇ **Oven:** Mix 250 mL water with 125 mL cloudy ammonia in an oven-proof bowl and place in warm oven for 10-15 minutes (oven off). Wipe off grime with a stiff brush and bicarbonate of soda, then wipe with a damp cloth.

◇ **Benches and table tops:** Use bicarbonate of soda, scourer and a damp cloth to wipe.

◇ **Stainless steel sink:** Rub with bicarbonate of soda on a damp cloth.

◇ **Painted surfaces:** Dissolve 1 tablespoon Borax in boiling water added to soapy water.

◇ **Tiles:** Use white vinegar on a cloth to wipe down greasy tiles.

◇ **Dishwashing by hand:** Hot water and pure soap will remove grease in soft-water areas. Add washing soda in hard-water areas. Use soda and soap dissolved in boiling water for more ingrained dirt.

◇ **Automatic dishwasher:** Washing soda can be used instead of commercial brands of detergent. For rinse aids, vinegar will reduce spotting and streaking.

◇ **Fridge:** Clean with warm water and soap. To deodorise, wipe down with vanilla essence or leave an open packet of bicarbonate of soda in the fridge.

◇ **Glass:** If you live in a hard-water area you may get spotting on glass. Just add vinegar to the final rinse – this works well for windows too.

◇ **Jars:** To rid jars of musty smells, fill half way with water and add 1 tablespoon of dry mustard. Shake well and stand for 20 minutes then rinse thoroughly. Or put 1 tablespoon each of tea leaves and vinegar in the jar, fill with warm water and stand for 2-3 hours. Rinse well.

◇ **Kettles:** Boiling equal parts of vinegar and water in the kettle will remove hard water encrustation. A few clean pebbles added to the water will help to break up thick deposits.

◇ **Ovens:** To clean, make a paste of bicarbonate of soda and water and apply to the inside of a warm oven with a spatula. Leave to dry and then clean off with a stiff brush and very hot water. Wipe the newly cleaned oven with a solution of 1 heaped tablespoon of bicarbonate of soda and 300 mL of water to make cleaning easier next time. Try to keep your oven reasonably clean by wiping it out after each use. To clean oven racks, soak in washing soda dissolved in water.

◇ **Stainless steel:** Dip a dry cloth in plain flour or cornflour and wipe over for a good shine. Heat marks can be removed by rubbing with a scouring pad and lemon juice.

◇ **Copper:** Rub with vinegar using a soft cloth. Polish with a dry cloth.

◇ **Chrome:** Polish with cider vinegar, or dip a dry cloth in ordinary flour and wipe over.

◇ **Brass:** Shine brass using a paste of vinegar and salt. Also try lemon juice or white wine vinegar mixed with bicarbonate of soda, or Worcestershire sauce.

◇ **Pewter:** Polish with the outer leaves of a cabbage and then buff with a soft cloth.

◇ **Silver:** Make a solution of one part washing soda to 20 parts water and put into an aluminium pan (the bubbles created by doing this are not toxic). Dip the silver into mixture then rinse in hot water and dry with a clean soft cloth. Or soak silver for 10-15 minutes in a saucepan containing hot water, a few aluminium bottle tops or a piece of aluminium foil and 1 tablespoon of washing soda.

◇ **Sinks:** Clean and disinfect your sink by scouring with salt.

◇ **Stains:** Different types of food stains, such as egg on cutlery or vegetable juice on bench tops, can be removed by dipping a damp cloth into table salt or bicarbonate of soda and then rubbing it firmly over the stain. Ashes can be used instead with the same results.

◇ **Tea stains:** Rub cups with lemon juice or salt.

◇ **Tiles:** If you apply a wax polish to ceramic tiles (see page 21) they will be easy to wipe down. For general cleaning, use bicarbonate of soda or a 50/50 water and vinegar mix.

❖ YOUR BATHROOM ❖

Your bathroom, like the kitchen, should be kept clean because it is a breeding ground for germs. This isn't very difficult to manage if you do a little gentle cleaning on a regular basis.

Try using a natural acid such as vinegar instead of commercial cleaners and bleachers when cleaning the bathroom. It will do as good a job but won't pollute the water when washed away.

◇ **Bath and basin:** Make a paste of bicarbonate of soda and water. Apply with a soft cloth, then wipe off with a moist cloth and rinse. Leave mixture on longer for stubborn stains.

◇ **Mould:** Wipe vinegar onto affected surfaces. Leave overnight and scrub off the next morning.

◇ **Tiles:** Use a paste of bicarbonate of soda or a 50/50 mixture of vinegar and water. If you apply a wax polish to your tiles they will be easier to wipe down.

◇ **Toilet:** To clean bowl, leave vinegar to soak for about 10 minutes. Limescale can then be easily scrubbed off. Flush toilets were specifically designed for hygiene without chemicals.

◇ **Chemical toilet cleaners:** Most toilet cleaners are poisonous so store out of reach of children and make sure lids are childproof, just in case. Bleach isn't a cleaning agent, it just bleaches surfaces and materials white. Eventually, it damages chrome, laminates and other plastic materials as well as the environment. Use vinegar and lemon juice instead. Don't mix your chemical cleaners as they can combine to form explosive or toxic gases.

❖ YOUR LAUNDRY ❖

Use pure soap powders in your laundry whenever possible. Avoid phosphate detergents as they pollute water and endanger water plants and wildlife. It's not that important for your clothes to be whiter than white.

◇ **Pure soap:** Pure soap or soap flakes do just as good a job as harsh powders or liquid detergents. To make your own washing powder: combine 1 cup of soap flakes with $1/_2$ cup of washing soda. In soft-water areas, use a greater proportion of soap flakes and, in hard-water areas, use more washing soda.

◇ **Detergent:** To remove detergent residues from clothes, just add $1/_2$ cup of washing soda to the machine and prewash. It's important to do this as detergent film may yellow your clothes when mixed with soap.

◇ **Machine washing:** Dissolve

soap flakes in a little hot water before adding them to the wash.

◇ **Streaking:** To prevent streaking in dark cottons and to prolong the life of stretch fabrics, add 125 mL of white vinegar to the rinse cycle.

◇ **Heavily soiled clothes:** Use a solution of $1^1/_2$ tablespoons washing soda in 250 mL warm water.

◇ **Soiled nappies:** Pre-soak in a solution of one part washing soda to four parts water.

HAND WASHING

◇ **Indian cotton:** Wash in cold water. Add a handful of salt or 125 mL of vinegar to the water to

ensure the colours don't run. Don't soak. Drip dry.

◇ **Lace:** Wash in warm, soapy water by squeezing and kneading. Rinse in warm water.

◇ **Linen:** Wash in lukewarm water using pure soap flakes.

◇ **Silk:** Wash in cold water using a mild pure soap or soap flakes. Rinse well and allow to drip dry. Iron while still slightly damp. To restore the sheen to silk, add white wine vinegar to the final rinse.

◇ **Woollens:** Wash in cool or lukewarm water with pure soap or soap flakes. Squeeze out in a towel and dry flat.

WASHING POWDER

If you want to use a commercial washing powder, choose one that is phosphate-free, 100% biodegradable and packaged in paper. Try halving the amount recommended on the packet.

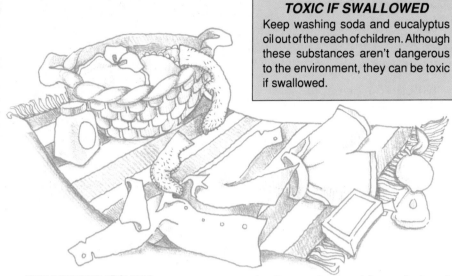

REMOVING STAINS

The key is quick action and identification.

◇ **Ballpoint pen:** As soon as this happens, sponge with methylated spirits, then flush repeatedly in cold water.

◇ **Blood:** Soak in cold, salted water for 10 minutes and then wash with soap. For really stubborn stains, apply a mixture of cornflour, talcum powder or cornmeal (polenta) mixed with water. Allow to dry; brush off.

◇ **Cosmetics:** Rub with glycerine and wash with warm, soapy water and washing soda.

◇ **Coffee:** Wash out with cool water then vinegar and rinse. Or mix egg yolk with lukewarm water and rub on stain.

◇ **Chewing gum:** Put item in freezer until gum freezes and is easily loosened.

◇ **Crayon on wall paper:** Press a piece of white bread into the stain to absorb the grease and colour. White toothpaste will also remove crayon from washable wall paper.

◇ **Fruit:** Cover stain immediately with salt and soak in milk before washing.

◇ **Glue:** Many glue stains can be removed by dabbing with eucalyptus oil.

◇ **Grass:** Soak with methylated spirits, allow to dry, then wash.

◇ **Grease spots:** If the spot is fresh, sprinkle with bicarbonate of soda, leave for a few minutes then brush off. If grease spot has dried, wet the fabric and rub bicarbonate of soda into the spot. If it is a stubborn stain, repeat and leave for a few hours, then wash. Alternatively, if the fabric can take a hot iron, place brown paper over the stain and press for a few moments with a hot iron. The paper will absorb the grease. Wash garment in warm soapy water.

◇ **Ink:** Soak in milk.

◇ **Linen spots:** Rub spots with bicarbonate of soda and lemon juice before washing.

◇ **Lipstick:** Rub with cold cream or shortening and wash with washing soda. Or soak stain in milk for 30 minutes and then wash in warm, soapy water.

◇ **Mildew:** Pour strong soap and salt on the spots and place in sunlight. Keep the spots moist and repeat as often as necessary. Another method is to hang the article outside in direct sunlight – this will help kill the fungus.

◇ **Mustard:** Rub with glycerine, leave for 3-4 hours, and then wash with soap and cold water.

◇ **Nappies:** After scraping off the excess, soak soiled nappies in a strong solution of bicarbonate of soda dissolved in warm water. For stubborn stains, repeat several times. Wash in warm, soapy water, rinse well and dry in the sun.

◇ **Perfume:** Rub with glycerine, leave for 3-4 hours, and then wash with soap and cold water.

◇ **Perspiration odours:** Dissolve 2 heaped tablespoons of bicarbonate of soda in 6 litres of lukewarm water. Soak garment for an hour, then wash as usual.

◇ **Perspiration:** Soak in water with a good dollop of white wine vinegar or a handful of bicarbonate of soda. Try both and see which one works for you (this will depend on your body chemistry).

◇ **Raspberry (berry fruit):** Wash with soapy water and then rub lemon juice over the stain. Leave for an hour before rinsing.

◇ **Rust:** Saturate with lemon juice or sour milk and cover with salt or bicarbonate of soda. Allow to dry then wash in warm, soapy water.

◇ **Scorch:** Rub well with white wine vinegar and rinse with cold water.

◇ **Tea and cocoa:** Rub with glycerine, leave for 3-4 hours and then wash with soap and cold water.

◇ **Wax:** To remove wax from fabric, place a block of ice onto wax, or place in freezer. Scrape off after 2 hours.

◇ **Wine:** Soda water is excellent for removing white wine stains. Pour the soda water through the stain, then wash. For old stains, leave glycerine on for 20 minutes before washing. For red wine, pour salt on immediately, let it stand for a while, then soak in cold water and rub out.

❖ GENERAL CLEANING TIPS ❖

By using salt, soda and soap and a little elbow grease, you can help lessen the damage to our environment. What better time to start than the present?

ALL-PURPOSE CLEANER

- ☐ **50 mL vinegar**
- ☐ **120 mL bicarbonate of soda**
- ☐ **50 mL cloudy ammonia**

Mix ingredients in 4 litres of hot water. This is a safe solution for all areas and can be rinsed off with water. Put the solution in a simple pump-action spray bottle or pour straight on to your cleaning cloth. Shake the mixture well before use. Avoid inhaling ammonia vapour.

◇ **Cane:** Wipe cane over with a solution of equal parts vinegar and water. Dry out of doors, if possible, on a warm day.

◇ **Carpets:** To deodorise and fully clean carpets, mix one part borax (a natural salt) with two parts cornmeal. Sprinkle liberally, leave for about an hour and vacuum. If you have some tough stains, blot with vinegar in soapy water. For quick deodorising, sprinkle the carpet with bicarbonate of soda, then vacuum.

◇ **Disinfectant:** Pure tea-tree oil is a natural and effective disinfectant. It can be added to your general cleaners, and is also a handy antiseptic for cuts or bites.

◇ **Lino or tile floors:** Use the All-purpose cleaner (see recipe). If you want a lemon-fresh smell, add a tablespoon of lemon essence to the rinse water. You can also use a soap, vinegar and water solution for washing floors.

◇ **Floor polish:** Use bees wax to polish. Or melt 1 tablespoon of paraffin wax in a double boiler then add a few drops of lemon essence and apply with a rag. Allow to dry then polish.

◇ **Furniture polish:** Rub with a mixture of olive oil and lemon juice or wipe over with a chamois leather wrung out in water and vinegar. Polish with a soft, dry cloth. Or dissolve 1 teaspoon of lemon oil in 1 pint of mineral oil and apply with a rag.

◇ **Heat marks on furniture:** Rub with a paste of olive oil or vegetable oil plus salt or cigarette ash. Remove paste and give the piece a coat of wax polish.

◇ **Leather:** Remove stains from leather using a solution of vinegar and warm water. To finish, rub over with olive oil.

◇ **Mirrors:** Use 125 mL of white vinegar mixed with 1 litre of water. Rub dry with a newspaper for an even finish.

◇ **Wood:** A few drops of vinegar in 250 mL of water is enough for daily or weekly use (60 mL of vinegar to 1 litre of water if you are making a large batch). Dip the cloth in this mixture and wring it out until it is just damp. Run it over the polished surface then buff with a soft cloth. For more thorough and less frequent polishing, mix two parts vegetable oil or olive oil with one part lemon juice. Shake mixture well before use.

◇ **Varnished surfaces:** Wipe over with strained cold tea.

◇ **Vinyl upholstery:** Wash with a strong solution of cider vinegar then rinse and dry well.

◇ **Wallpaper:** Remove all dust with a feather duster or vacuum cleaner. Wipe the wall down with 2-day-old, thick slices of bread. For vinyl wallpaper, clean with a warm cloth and white vinegar.

◇ **Windows:** Use a solution of 125 mL of white vinegar and 1 litre of water. Rub dry to avoid streaking. If windows are very grubby, wash with soapy water first.

STORING CLOTHES

Dry cleaning is bad for your clothes as well as the environment because it relies on chemicals to do the job. One of the best ways to avoid dry cleaning is to store your clothes properly.

◇ Air suits outside or in an unoccupied room after wearing. All tailored clothing should be hung on well-padded, shaped hangers.

◇ Make sure cotton is properly dry after washing to prevent mildew in storage.

◇ Wrap white cottons and linens in blue tissue to stop yellowing and store away from strong light.

◇ Rinse synthetic fabrics in cool water to prevent creases. Let pleated fabrics drip dry into shape before folding them for storage.

◇ Keep silk in a cool, dry and dark place – strong light will fade the dye.

◇ Never store suedes and leather in plastic bags. Always store somewhere cool and well ventilated.

◇ Don't crowd clothing hung in your wardrobe – leave space between hangers so garments can breathe and stay free of creases.

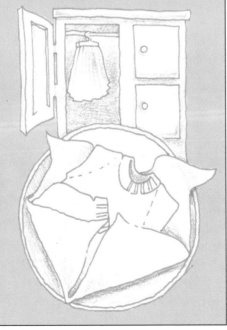

❖ AIR FRESHENERS ❖

Although strong odours can be unpleasant they are usually quite harmless, unlike aerosol sprays which harm the environment. Fresh air is the best air freshener, so keep your home well ventilated at all times. Indoor plants, scented or not, will help keep the air fresh because they absorb carbon dioxide and release oxygen.

When you do want to disguise a bad smell or add a pleasant scent, use natural air fresheners like flowers or herbs. Throughout history pot pourris have been used to freshen rooms.

Air fresheners don't rid your home of odours – they are designed to either mask smells with another strong odour or to inhibit your ability to smell. This is done by coating the inside of your nostrils with a film of oil or chemically altering your sense of smell.

COOKING SMELLS

◇ **Strong cooking smells** can be overwhelming. Always cook with your windows open or at least make sure your kitchen is well ventilated.

◇ **Apple** will help combat strong food smells. A slice of apple in the pan when you fry fish will tone down the smell.

◇ If you are **steaming cabbage** or brussels sprouts, place a crust of bread over the top of the vegetables, then cover tightly.

◇ **Lemon and vinegar** have good deodorising qualities. Both can be rubbed over hands to get rid of smells like onion or garlic.

◇ **A bowl of white wine vinegar** placed next to the stove when you are frying will cut

down on the smell and smoke. Leave a bowl permanently by the stove – as the vinegar evaporates it will deodorise the air.

◇ **If you've burnt something** in the kitchen, boil a few pieces of lemon in a small saucepan of water to clear the air. Boiling cloves and cinnamon also works.

POT POURRI

Pot pourri can be made from many different leaves, herbs and flowers in your chosen combination. Many pot pourri flowers have colours which tend to fade when the petals dry. Some of the unscented kinds retain their colours and for this reason are worth including to make your pot pourri mixture more appealing. Pot geranium petals, for example, keep their colours well, so collect and keep any which fall.

Pot pourri scents vary according to the ingredients. One made mostly of rose petals will differ from one made of lavender, marigolds or verbena.

To retain their strength flower scents must be fixed. The ingredients for use as fixatives vary. Coarse sea salt is one, another is dried and powdered citrus peel. Dry orange, tangerine and lemon peel in a cool oven or keep in a warm, dry place until peel is hard enough to be ground or pounded to a powder. Angelica root powder can also be used.

Once you've made your selection, dry the different ingredients separately (tie in bundles and either hang to dry or lay out on a wire-mesh rack and turn regularly).

When properly dried, put your herbs and flowers into a glass jar (never metal) and mix together. If you want a stronger scent, add a few drops of essential oil to the mixture. Cover tightly and leave for 3-6 weeks.

CITRUS POT POURRI
- [ ] **8 cups of a combination of any or all of the following: lemon, verbena, lemon-scented tea -tree, lemon thyme, lemon-scented geranium and/or lemon grass**
- [ ] **1 cup eau-de-cologne mint**
- [ ] **1 cup calendula petals**
- [ ] **1/2 cup each orange and lemon peel**
- [ ] **1 cup whole allspice, lightly crushed**
- [ ] **1 cup fixative**
- [ ] **6-8 drops lemon verbena oil**
- [ ] **3-4 drops bergamot oil**

Use dried daffodils, nasturtiums or everlasting daisies for decoration.

❖ HOUSEHOLD PESTS ❖

One of the best ways to prevent pests from taking over your home is to remove whatever is attracting them. Avoid using chemicals in the form of insecticides and sprays – these are unnecessary if you keep pests away in the first place. There are many common-sense, natural ways of dealing with household pests.

Try some of our safe, non-toxic methods for pest control.

Ants

◇ Find out where ants are coming in and sprinkle mint, chilli powder, pepper or borax across their trail.

◇ Put pennyroyal, rue or tansy in your kitchen cupboards or on shelves to keep them away.

◇ Plant mint near windows and doors as ants don't like the smell.

Ant nests

Mix one part borax with one part icing sugar. Scatter it over a piece of wood near the nest. The ants are attracted by the icing sugar. Borax will poison the ants but is harmless to humans and animals.

Cockroaches

◇ Make a mixture of flour, cocoa and borax and leave it out in shallow dishes.

◇ Bicarbonate of soda mixed with icing sugar can also be used. Make sure these are kept out of the reach of children and pets.

◇ Sprinkle cockroach-infested areas with pyrethrum powder (derived from the pyrethrum plant).

Fleas

Flea eggs can hatch in 2-12 days in warm conditions, but in cool temperatures may remain dormant for months.

◇ If fleas have invaded your home, you'll need to clean out the whole house, vacuum regularly and sprinkle oil of lavender or pennyroyal around infested rooms. Empty the vacuum cleaner after each use.

◇ Controlling fleas on your pets is the first step to preventing household infestations. Give pets herbal baths and use a flea comb regularly. Rub your pet with a mixture of olive oil and a few drops of lavender, thyme, pennyroyal or eucalyptus oil. Wash your pet's bedding and replace it with old cotton sheeting or paper.

GENERAL TIPS

◇ Store food in airtight containers – preferably glass.

◇ Don't leave crumbs or food lying around uncovered.

◇ Wipe down bench tops and stoves after use.

◇ Don't leave dirty dishes in the sink.

◇ Empty bins regularly and keep them clean.

◇ Don't keep stagnant water near the house.

◇ Install fly and mosquito screens where necessary.

❖ HOW TO MAKE A POMANDER ❖

The original pomander consisted of a strongly scented pot pourri, formed into a ball with fragrant gum or wax and worn round the neck or waist in a small, perforated container. It was thought to ward off diseases.

The following instructions are for making an orange pomander which can be hung in the wardrobe, put into a linen drawer or placed in a pot pourri jar. It should keep its scent for several years.

MATERIALS
- ☐ **a small thin-skinned orange, free from blemishes**
- ☐ **a darning needle or fine skewer**
- ☐ **about 25 g of cloves**
- ☐ **1 teaspoon each of powdered cinnamon and orris root**
- ☐ **a little freshly grated nutmeg and ground ginger**
- ☐ **grease-proof paper or a paper bag**
- ☐ **30 cm of narrow ribbon**

To make the pomander

Prick holes in the orange peel using a darning needle and leaving a cross pattern round which you will eventually tie the ribbon. Make the holes fairly close together, and do not go so deep as to let the juice run out.

Stick cloves in the holes so the spaces between the cross are covered completely. Mix together ground cinnamon and orris root. Roll the orange in the mixture, rubbing and patting the powder in. Add a little freshly grated nutmeg and ground ginger if you wish.

Wrap the orange in grease-proof paper or put into a brown paper bag. Leave it in a cool, dark place for 5-6 weeks or until it is hard and dry. Shake off any loose powder and tie the pomander round with ribbon. Make sure the pomander stays dry – this will ensure the best results over a long period of time.

Flies

◇ Keep all food and garbage covered and clean the rubbish bin regularly.

◇ Don't place your compost heap or piles of manure close to the house.

◇ Hang up sprigs of lavender, mint, pennyroyal, or rue to keep flies away. Rub the leaves often to release the smell. These herbs can also be planted near windows and doors or in pots in the kitchen.

◇ Install fine mesh fly screens where necessary.

Mice

◇ Hang sprigs of mint or tansy in your kitchen cupboards or on shelves.

◇ Block up possible entry holes in the pantry or in cupboards under the sink.

◇ Keep all food in containers.

◇ Cover all rubbish tightly.

Moths

◇ Moths don't like the smell of lavender – hence the old-fashioned lavender bag. Natural camphor or cloves, mint, sage, wormwood and rosemary will also prove effective.

◇ Clean all clothes, bedding and furnishing fabrics before storing them – moths breed in dust and dirt.

◇ Rid clothes of moth eggs by hanging them in the sun for a few hours or putting them through the clothes dryer.

◇ Clean out drawers, wardrobes and chests from time to time,

NATURAL PEST CONTROL	
PESTS	**HERBS**
ants	tansy, pennyroyal, rue, spearmint, pepper-mint (effective inside and outside the home)
aphids	nasturtiums, pennyroyal
borers	garlic, nasturtiums
clothes moths	mint, sage, lavender, wormwood, rosemary (hang fresh bunches where needed or fill sachets with dried herbs)
caterpillars	mint, wormwood, garlic, chives
cockroaches	pyrethrum
eel worms, greenfly, whitefly	marigolds
fleas	fennel, wormwood, lavender, thyme, pennyroyal
flies	basil, tansy, chamomile, wormwood, pyrethrum, lavender, mint, pennyroyal, rue
mice	spearmint, tansy
mosquitoes	pennyroyal, basil, mint, chamomile, tansy (rub yourself with the leaves)
red spider mites	lemon grass, coriander, garlic, chives
cabbage moth and butterfly	mint, rosemary, dill
silverfish	rosemary
cats and dogs	rue (plant as a border around flower beds)

checking clothes for any signs of moths.

Mosquitoes

Mosquitoes breed in standing water and multiply very quickly.

◇ Cover all water vessels and rain gutters.

◇ Garden ponds or swimming pools should be located away from the house.

◇ Use slow-burning mosquito rings or coils (made of pyrethrum). Keep windows shut for best results.

◇ Hang mosquito nets above beds to keep mosquitoes out. Install fine mesh mosquito screens on your windows and doors.

◇ Also try pennyroyal, basil, mint, chamomile or tansy as natural repellents (rub yourself with the leaves)

Mites

Mites attack the soft, warm parts of the body and bite, causing itching and swelling.

◇ Keep bird cages clean.

◇ Dust and vacuum regularly to prevent mites.

Weevils and food moths

Small moths in your cupboards are a sign of weevils and food moths. Check the dried food in your cupboards regularly.

◇ Place a bay leaf in your food containers to keep weevils and food moths from laying eggs in flour, rice and pulses.

INSECT REPELLENTS

Try the following:

◇ **Vinegar** rubbed on exposed skin. The smell will disappear as it dries but the taste will linger and insects find it repellent.

◇ **Citronella** (although some people find the smell hard to take, it compares favourably with commercial brands).

◇ **Vegetable oil** that has been infused with pennyroyal.

◇ **Tea-tree oil** rubbed on the skin.

❖ JUST FOR YOU ❖

Many of the toiletries and cosmetics you use everyday for personal hygiene contain detergents and chemicals that are harmful to the environment.
There are literally thousands of brands of shampoos, deodorants, toothpastes, creams, lotions and potions to choose from. Some you buy from the supermarket, others only from department stores or very exclusive salons.
When you buy toiletries or cosmetics, look for simple ingredients and packaging. Better still, why not try our natural, homemade recipes?

NATURAL BEAUTY CARE

Look for natural beauty care products which have been produced from 100 per cent pure plant, herbal and mineral ingredients.

☐ not animal tested, no animal ingredients
☐ allergy free and environmentally safe
☐ no CFCs and therefore ozone friendly
☐ 100 per cent biodegradable (containers recyclable)
☐ petrochemical free, safe for septic systems

HAIR CARE

Keep hair and scalp clean and healthy the natural way.

Nourishing egg shampoo

Beat 1 egg yolk, then slowly beat in 250 mL of water. Work mixture well into your scalp and hair using fingertips. Rinse thoroughly and dry.

Egg and lemon shampoo

Make shampoo by blending juice of 1 lemon with 1 egg yolk. This gives a natural gloss to your hair.

HAIRSPRAY

Combine 2 chopped lemons and 500 mL of water in a pot and simmer until lemons are soft. Cool and strain. Put into a pump-action spray bottle and store in the fridge. If you prefer to keep it at room temperature, add a shot of vodka as a preservative. If the mixture is too sticky, add more water.

Family shampoo

Save all your leftover pieces of soap or grate a fresh bar. Boil in 500 mL of water and simmer till the soap has dissolved. When mixture has cooled, pour into a wide-mouthed container. A few drops of essential oil can be added for fragrance. When the mixture is cold it will form a jelly.

Conditioners for dry hair

◇ Add a couple of teaspoons of plain yoghurt to the final rinse after shampooing.

◇ Shampoo your hair, rinse and towel-dry then apply about a tablespoon of mayonnaise to your scalp. Work it through thoroughly and leave it on for about an hour. Shampoo your hair once more using as little shampoo as possible, then rinse.

◇ For very dry hair, warm a small amount of almond, olive or peanut oil by putting it in a cup in a bowl of hot water. When the oil is warm, apply it to your scalp using finger tips or a wad of cotton. Ensure a good spread by continually parting your hair and patting the oil along the parts. Dip a towel in hot water, wring it out and wrap it around your head. When the towel cools, redip it in hot water and apply again. Do this about three times over a half-hour period, then shampoo and rinse your hair.

Hair rinse for shine

Add vinegar or lemon juice to the final rinse – this removes all traces of shampoo and adds a lustrous shine. Vinegar is recommended for brunettes, lemon juice for blondes. Use the citrus rinse if you have very oily hair.

ROSEMARY HERB RINSE

Strip the rosemary leaves from the stems. Place a heaped tablespoonful in a jug and pour on 300 mL of boiling water. Allow to steep for quarter of an hour. Strain. Use the strained liquid as a final rinse after washing the hair.

Herbal rinses

To prepare herbal rinses, boil a handful of your chosen herbs in 500 mL of water, bring to the boil, cool, then strain. Or place a handful of herbs in the bottom of a bowl, pour boiling water over them, allow to cool and strain. You can make any herbal rinse this way. Make a large batch at a time. Here are a few suggestions for herbal rinses: chamomile for blondes, sage for brunettes, rosemary for fragrance and lustre, thyme for fragrance and lavender for fragrance and to condition the scalp.

Dandruff

If you suffer from dandruff, first look at your diet and general health. You may have a vitamin B deficiency.

◇ Quite often dandruff is stress related. In this case, relaxation techniques will be far more effective than medicated shampoos.

◇ Rub bicarbonate of soda into dry hair to help clear up dandruff. Massage a good handful into your hair and scalp, and rinse thoroughly in clear water.

◇ Strong herbal hair rinses including rosemary, thyme or sage will also help.

EYE CARE
Eye cleanser
A warm, lightly salted water bath is the most soothing treatment for sore eyes. To make a water bath, dissolve 1 teaspoon of salt in 500 mL of water. Allow the liquid to cool. Apply to your eyes using an eye cup, a cupped hand, an eye dropper or a dab of cottonwool. Blink the liquid around your eyes.

Pick-me-up for tired eyes
Add 3 teaspoons of tea leaves to 250 mL of warm water. Dab the solution onto your eyes using a cotton ball.

Soothing compress
Use grated raw potato. Put grated potato between 2 layers of gauze or fine cotton and place over your eyes. Lie down for 15 minutes for the best results.

Eyelash conditioner
Condition your eyelashes from time to time by applying a little almond or olive oil to them.

SUNBURN TIPS

◇ Plain yoghurt applied to burnt areas is very soothing. Just spread it on straight from the fridge, leave it for a while and rinse off in warm water.

◇ Vinegar rubbed over burnt areas gives relief.

◇ Rub raw cucumber over sunburn or make a lotion by peeling and mashing the cucumber and mixing it with a little milk.

LIPS, TEETH AND GUMS
Lips
Use almond oil to keep your lips smooth and free from chapping.

Teeth
Give your teeth a special clean by using a mixture of bicarbonate of soda and lemon juice. Mix these two ingredients into a smooth paste and use in place of toothpaste. Rinse out with cool water.

A mixture of bicarbonate of soda and water will bring your teeth to a brilliant white. A few

---

HAND CARE
Lemon juice
Lemon juice is good for whitening nails and will help get rid of excess cuticle.

Olive oil
A few drops of olive oil are all you need to keep your hands soft and smooth. Add some salt to the olive oil if your hands are particularly dry and rough. Rub hands together and work the mixture gently into your skin for a few minutes. Wash off with pure soap and warm water. This mixture can also be used on other rough spots like elbows or feet.

Oatmeal
Oatmeal is a good soap substitute. Pour some into your cupped hand and add enough water to make a rough paste. Rub gently over your hands in a washing motion and rinse off with tepid water.

Chapped hands
If your hands are chapped, rinse them with a little vinegar every time you wash. Don't rinse the vinegar off, just pat dry – the smell soon fades. Or try rubbing chapped hands with the yellow side of lemon peel, then rinse and dry thoroughly.

---

drops of peppermint oil can be added for a minty flavour.

Gums
Dissolve $\frac{1}{2}$ teaspoon of salt in a half glass of water as a naturally cleansing mouthwash. This is also good to use after dental work or if you have sore gums. In these cases, make the solution a bit stronger – try 2-3 teaspoons of salt in a glass of warm water. Eating raw crunchy vegetables is also good for keeping gums in good condition.

Glycerine
A drop of glycerine worked into the skin gives a protective covering to the hands. Hands must be dry when glycerine is applied.

Hand lotion
Combine equal parts of strained ripe tomato, glycerine and lemon juice. Rub this mixture into your hands for a few minutes – rinse with tepid water. Or mix equal amounts of honey, lemon juice, glycerine and olive oil together. Keep in a sealed bottle.

SUGAR

If you've spent the day in the garden or cleaning out the garage you'll find the dirt comes off more easily if you add a tablespoon of sugar to your handwashing water.

BATHS

There are times when your tired body screams out for a long soak in the bath. Try our natural preparations to help soothe those aching muscles and calm frayed nerves or just to pamper yourself.

Oil bath: All sorts of oils can be added to your bath. Try olive oil, almond or vegetable oil. These are good for dry skin or after a day in the sun. Aromatic oils can be very relaxing (see recipe).

Oatmeal bath: An oatmeal bath is soothing and cleansing. Tie your oatmeal in a piece of fabric or put it in the toe of a sock and place in the bath while you run the water. Rub it over your skin for best results.

Milk bath: Milk softens and smoothes the skin. Add a glassful to the bath water.

Milk baths are also good for sunburn.

Salt bath: A handful of salt added to your bath water is cleansing and toning.

Herbal bath: Herbal mixtures are very relaxing and produce a beautiful fragrance. Tie herbs in a piece of cloth and place in the bath while you are running the water.

Bath bags: Dry and mix thoroughly in equal quantities lemon balm, rosemary, lavender leaves or flower spikes, eau de cologne and pineapple mint, philadelphus flowers or whatever else is available. Make small bags or sachets of muslin or fine net, filled with the mixture and fasten. Throw the bags into a hot bath to scent the water.

AROMATIC BATH OILS

Use strongly scented flowers like
- ☐ **roses**
- ☐ **lavender**

and therapeutic herbs like
- ☐ **rosemary**
- ☐ **lemon verbena**
- ☐ **chamomile**
- ☐ **mint**
- ☐ **thyme**

Pour 1.5 litres of light, non-smelling oil into a large bowl. Add as many flowers or herbs as the bowl will hold and saturate the petals or leaves. Allow to soak for 24 hours. Remove flowers or herbs with slotted spoon and discard. Add more fresh flowers or herbs to oil. Repeat with 6 batches of flowers or herbs, then strain liquid through cheesecloth.

DEODORANT TIP

Bicarbonate of soda is an excellent anti-perspirant. Apply with cotton wool after your bath or shower while your skin is still slightly damp. Rub some essential oil under your arms after bathing.

FEET
Soothing foot bath
Soak your feet in a few litres of warm water mixed with a cup of bicarbonate of soda or salt. Alternating your feet between hot and cold foot baths for 10-20 minutes is also soothing.

Swollen feet
Cut a potato in half and rub over your feet in a circular motion. Let the potato juice dry and leave overnight. This will help reduce swelling.

Thyme foot bath
Foot baths are both refreshing and restorative. Pick a handful of fresh thyme or if only dried thyme is available, use 3 tablespoons. Have your small tub ready and add 1 tablespoon of thyme and 1 tablespoon of sea salt. Pour in enough boiling water to cover the feet. Allow this to cool until comfortably warm, then soak your feet in it.

ACHES AND PAINS
Dilute wintergreen oil (also known as methylsalicilate) with a rubbing oil such as almond or safflower, and massage into sore muscles to ease the pain. Only use a small amount of wintergreen oil as it burns, and also smells very strong. It has a very powerful deep action and can unlock stiff muscles. You may prefer to use rosemary oil, which calms the nerves and eases muscle pain. Lavender and marjoram oil are also effective for stiff muscles and rheumatic pain. For gout and rheumatism, a regular diet of chives and chervil is said to ease the pain.

POULTICES
A poultice is a preparation of chopped or crushed herbs wrapped in muslin and applied to a sore spot as hot as you can bear it. Poultices draw the poisons out of infected areas, soothe inflammations and promote healing.
◇ Place herbs in the centre of a piece of muslin, twist it up and tie with string, then dunk herb bag into a bowl of boiling water.
◇ Squeeze out any excess moisture and apply immediately to the sore spot. Hold it there until it cools or bandage it in position.

FACIAL TREATMENTS
Cleansing
Milk is an excellent facial cleanser for delicate skins. Apply with cotton wool and leave for a few minutes. Rinse off in lukewarm water.

Deep cleansing
Pour boiling water into a bowl and add the herb of your choice. Lean your face over the steam and cover head and bowl with a towel. Use mint leaves for toning and refreshing, chamomile to cleanse and calm, lemon peel and juice for a more astringent blend. This deep cleansing method is best for oily skins.

Olive oil
Work a small amount of olive oil (almond oil can also be used) into your skin using finger tips.

Fruit packs
To make a fruit pack, mash fruit to a pulp and apply it. Leave pack on for 15-20 minutes then remove with warm water. Following are some recommended fruits and their benefits:
◇ Lemons – astringent and drying (good for oily skins)
◇ Oranges – soothing and restful
◇ Melon – cooling and refreshing
◇ Cucumber – astringent and cooling
◇ Bananas – soothing and softening
◇ Strawberries – toning
◇ Tomatoes – cleansing

Many herbal teas have a soothing, refreshing or stimulating effect. They can be drunk hot or cold. Usually the leaves or flowers of the herb are used to make the tea but occasionally seeds are used. Crush seeds with a pestle and mortar before use.

Sage tea is a popular gargle to soothe a sore throat. Lemon balm leaves make a fragrant tea which soothes and calms. Drink fennel tea to stimulate the appetite and improve digestion.

◇ If using dried herbs, add 1 teaspoon to each cup (250 mL) of boiling water.

◇ If using fresh herbs, lightly crush, chop, or bruise before putting into the teapot.

◇ Use a china teapot, and leave the infusion to steep for 5-6 minutes.

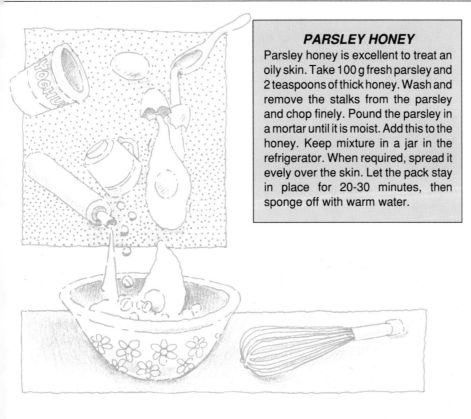

PARSLEY HONEY

Parsley honey is excellent to treat an oily skin. Take 100 g fresh parsley and 2 teaspoons of thick honey. Wash and remove the stalks from the parsley and chop finely. Pound the parsley in a mortar until it is moist. Add this to the honey. Keep mixture in a jar in the refrigerator. When required, spread it evely over the skin. Let the pack stay in place for 20-30 minutes, then sponge off with warm water.

Facial masks

◇ Beat together 1 egg yolk and 1 tablespoon of olive oil. Smooth mixture over your face and leave for about 20 minutes. Wash off with warm water and pat dry.

◇ Smooth on plain yoghurt and leave for 15 minutes. Wash off with warm water.

◇ Mix 1 cup of oatmeal, 60 mL of water and 2 tablespoons of honey to a paste. Apply all over your face. Leave to dry then rinse off with warm water.

◇ Beat 2 teaspoons of lemon juice, 1 egg yolk and 1 teaspoon of honey till it thickens. Apply and leave for about 10 minutes or until dry. Rinse off with cool water.

USE IT AGAIN
RECYCLE

- ❖ Recycling
- ❖ Trash equals cash
- ❖ Cutting down on waste
- ❖ Preparing to recycle
- ❖ Plastics
- ❖ Solar bags
- ❖ Mixed materials
- ❖ One-way containers
- ❖ The story of aluminium
- ❖ Organic waste

The rapid rise in the cost of garbage disposal heralds a brighter future for recycling.

FACT

In the USA, 90 per cent of the refuse is still being buried. Over 200,000 hectares are needed annually for this and space is now at a premium.

❖ RECYCLING ❖

Recycling is not only a more cost-effective means of disposing of waste, it may just turn the tide on global environmental problems and become one of the major growth industries of the 21st century!

This section is about recycling and how you can help turn the tide. There are lots of great tips, including how to convert your trash into cash and your organic waste into rich soil for the garden.

Water comes out of a tap, sewage is flushed down the toilet, garbage goes into plastic bins and vanishes overnight and food comes in containers from supermarkets – these are everyday, taken-for-granted events for many people.

Awareness of recycling helps to put you in touch with a

different reality – one which makes you more aware of what happens to these things when they come out the other end.

A SHORT HISTORY

Around 500 BC the Greeks introduced the first laws against dumping garbage in the streets. Municipal dumping areas were organised in Athens no less than 2 kilometres from the city walls. Unfortunately this practice of waste removal disappeared in medieval Europe, where garbage was again dumped in the streets and thrown out of windows.

10 GOLDEN RULES

◆ **Separate your garbage for recycling**
◆ **Compost your food scraps**
◆ **Use things until they are really worn out**
◆ **Buy milk in glass bottles instead of cartons**
◆ **Be wary of the disposable tag on products – how can you dispose of them?**
◆ **Avoid plastic**
◆ **Buy recycled paper**
◆ **Reuse envelopes, plastic bags and containers**
◆ **Take your own shopping bag or basket**
◆ **Choose biodegradable packaging**

After the industrial revolution, garbage was piled up in the countryside outside cities. As the cities grew and the countryside shrank, rat infestations and noxious odours became intolerable. Pits were dug in an attempt to confine the waste.

The first incineration of municipal waste was tested in England in 1874. Although the burning of waste could reduce its volume by 70 per cent to 90 per cent, the cost of incinerators was prohibitive, and many people opposed this method when their air quality deteriorated. Burying waste once again became the preferred choice.

DO THE RIGHT THING

Litter is a major problem the world over, not just because it's unsightly – IT KILLS. Thousands of sea mammals, birds and other wildlife species are killed annually by becoming ensnared in plastic or ingesting it.

◇ Always **take a litter bag** if you are spending the day outdoors.

◇ **Never throw rubbish out** the car windows – hang a litter bag from your dashboard or keep a box in the back.

◇ **If you see someone littering** go up and tell them politely that they have dropped something.

◇ **Pick up litter**, even if it isn't yours.

◇ **Report littering** – if you witness any major dumping of waste, report it to the authorities. There's no point in saying 'I don't want any trouble' or 'I don't want to get involved' – you already are! Litter affects everyone's lives.

BUYING RECYCLED

Recycling is a major step towards a sustainable future and needs your participation to work. One of the most important contributions you can make to it's future, apart from recycling your own waste, is to buy products that use recycled material in their manufacture.

Talk to your friends about buying recycled, particularly those in business who buy large quantities of paper or other resources.

WHY RECYCLE?

◇ **Save energy:** Every time energy is used up, so are vital, non-renewable resources. The energy used to produce the metal for one aluminium can is the same as that needed to recycle twenty. The energy required to make 300 aluminium cans is equivalent to 3 weeks petrol for an average motorist.

◇ **Save resources:** Natural resources will last longer if you recycle instead of using raw materials – each tonne of recycled paper saves half a hectare of trees. Just recycling the print run of a Sunday edition of the *New York Times* would leave 75,000 trees standing.

◇ **Save money:** Rubbish collection costs are kept to a minimum. Recycling can reduce your household garbage by up to 80 per cent and this saves on collection costs. The reduced cost, combined with the money your local councils can make by selling the waste, means more money spent on improving your local area and community services.

◇ **Save space:** If waste is being recycled, the amount of land needed for tipping sites will be reduced. The average consumer produces about 1 tonne of waste annually – vast areas of land are needed to accommodate this.

◇ **Create jobs:** Recycling is a modern growth industry and in future will require ever greater numbers of people to collect and sort goods, and to work in industries which use recycled materials. The sale of recyclable materials can earn money for schools, clubs and charities.

◇ **Reduce pollution:** Recycling materials is more energy efficient than starting from scratch using virgin materials – this means a general reduction in air, water and land pollution from factories and tips.

FACT

Percentage of paper recycled:
Mexico   50%
Nigeria 2%
Philippines 16%
Japan 45%
Australia 28%
Netherlands 43%
Note: On average only 25% of the world's paper is currently recycled.

TRASH = CASH

◇ **Garage and car boot sales:** A garage or car boot sale is one of the best forms of recycling because it extends the life of items in their original form. What you consider junk may be a bargain hunter's discovery of the day. If you don't have time to organise your own garage sale, offer your boxes of junk to a local charity, hospital or school (they will be only too happy to add them to their white elephant stall at the next fete or fair).

◇ **Aluminium cans:** Aluminium companies buy these back at a per kilo price. Children can make extra pocket money by collecting them from parks, playing fields and beaches – this is a fun way to make your kids aware of litter and its impact on the environment.

In the UK, billions of aluminium drink cans are used each year but until recently only a small percentage of these were recycled. Recycling saves up to 95 per cent of the energy required to produce aluminium.

◇ **Scrap metal:** This is worth money. Ring your local scrap metal merchants for prices and guidelines.

❖ CUT DOWN ON WASTE ❖

Recycling is a great way to conserve resources – but an even better alternative is to not create the waste in the first place!

Two important ways to minimise the problem are:

1 Maximise the life of the product in its original form – use things until they are really worn out.

2 Reduce the amount of waste produced. This is a major consideration when you do your weekly shop.

Make your selections not only on the nutritional and dollar values of a product but also on the amount of packaging. Assess the product's disposability once it becomes garbage.

In industrial countries, packaging constitutes 30-50 per cent of household waste. That's why it's so important to think about the recycling potential of packaging at the time of purchase.

MAKE THINGS LAST

Here are just a few suggestions for ways you can extend the life of a product in its original form. Once you start thinking along these lines you'll probably come up with endless possibilities. Share any new ideas you have with your friends.

◇ **Start an 'Ecology Store'** in your home. Store reusable items such as paper, string, boxes, cartons, plastic containers, ribbons, wool and fabrics to provide materials as the need arises. Set aside a drawer or cupboard for this purpose and encourage the whole family to use it.

◇ **Write on both sides** of your note paper.

◇ **Reuse envelopes** by crossing out the old addresses or sticking a new address label on.

◇ Recycle your **scrap paper** by making your own beautiful paper (see How to make your own paper, page 9).

◇ Save **gift wrapping**, ribbons and string for reuse.

◇ **Reuse jam jars** – wash and use again for food storage, keeping nails in, pencil holders and for the children to use in all sorts of ways (to hold water and paintbrushes, for example).

◇ **Egg cartons** make perfect seedling trays.

◇ **Pass on magazines or books.** Pass them round the neighbourhood or drop them at your local hospital or nursing home.

◇ **Decorate old glass bottles** and jars by painting them. This was all the rage in Victorian times for keeping lavender water, bath salts and other toiletries in. Store herbed oils and vinegars in bottles. Seal with corks.

◇ **Revive old mascara** dispensers in hot water for a few minutes and lengthen their life.

◇ **Old toothbrushes** can be used for cleaning those small, hard-to-get-at places around the home.

◇ **Use old tyres as planters** – fill with topsoil and plant with tomatoes, strawberries or herbs.

◇ **Recycle children's clothes** (or your own for that matter) by swapping, selling or giving them away. These would make an excellent donation to the local church bazaar or school fete.

◇ **Reuse plastic bags** for wrapping sandwiches, keeping stockings tidy and snag-free and storing and freezing foods.

◇ **Start a household 'Ragbag'** for storing all your clean fabric discards in – torn sheet remnants, dressmaking leftovers, worn out T-shirts. These can be used for so many different jobs – applying waxes and cleaners, washing windows, cleaning the car, sopping up stains or lining a box or basket for a new puppy or kitten.

◇ Use the better, **not-so-worn-out remnants** from the Ragbag for making all kinds of useful and pretty things – patchwork quilts, rag dolls, doll's house accessories, pot holders, pillow slips.

◇ **Ask about replacement parts** and servicing when you purchase any new appliances.

◇ Learn to do **basic repairs** yourself. Everyone should be able to sew a straight seam or replace a button. Simple repairs can add years to the life of an item.

◇ Anticipate where certain things are going to wear out and protect them from the beginning. **A rug in the right place** will save wear and tear on a brand new carpet.

FACT

◇ In developed countries, the average consumer produces about 1 tonne of waste every year.

◇ Throw away an aluminium soft-drink can and you throw away the energy equivalent of half a can of petrol.

❖ PREPARING TO RECYCLE ❖

Most households discard two full bins of waste each week.
At least 80 per cent of this rubbish has good recycling potential.
Separation of different types of waste is crucial to any recycling
program, all you need is a sorting system.
Think of your laundry and the way you separate it into
sections – whites, heavy-duty, coloured and delicates.
You can use a similar principle to recycle!

Organic matter is the only type of waste that can be recycled by you in your own home. If you live in a unit or apartment you may have a friend or neighbour whose compost heap can accommodate extra.

Glass, paper and cardboard, metal and organic matter all have excellent recycling potential.

Your household waste is made up of:	
Glass	10%
Paper and card	30%
Metal	10%
Organic matter	30%
Plastic	8%
Miscellaneous	12%

Always try to reuse plastics instead of throwing them away The plastic recycling processes currently available can only deal with one type of plastic and there are about 64 plastics commonly in use! The task of sorting all of these plastics is so labour intensive that recycling is unrealistic at this stage.

Miscellaneous waste generally includes items composed of several different substances. This waste has little recycling potential as each item would have to be broken up and the individual materials separated.

FACT

Every tonne of crushed waste glass used saves the equivalent of 135 litres of oil and replaces 1.2 tonnes of raw material.

To make the most of your waste for recycling, separate and treat it in the following ways:

◇ **Food scraps:** Keep food scraps and other household wastes separate in the kitchen (a container with a lid is best for this), and deposit regularly onto your compost heap. Organic waste is valuable garden fertiliser and should never go out in the garbage. If you don't have a garden or a compost, share a friend or neighbour's. Keen gardeners will welcome the extra fertiliser. (Also see All about compost on page 63.)

◇ **Glass:** Remove the lids and tops before adding glass containers to your recycling bin. If the containers are returnable milk bottles, for example, take them back rather than recycle. Any type of glass container is suitable for recycling. Glass can effectively be recycled forever.

◇ **Paper:** Newspapers and any other paper products are suitable for recycling. Look out for packets lined with plastic as these can't be recycled. 'High quality' paper such as office, computer or any white paper that has very little inking is particularly sought after by paper millers. Paper is best stored in cardboard boxes for collection or tied with natural fibre string. Don't put paper for recycling into plastic bags.

◇ **Steel cans:** Rinse cans to remove food scraps and squash them flat.

◇ **Metal:** Keep all forms of scrap metal – it's worth money. Look up scrap merchants in your area and find out the current prices for scrap metal and guidelines for sorting.

◇ **Aluminium cans:** These are worth money! Your children will welcome the chance to earn extra pocket money and local charities will happily take them off your hands. Squash cans flat for collection. Some recycling

BENEFITS FROM USING RECYCLED MATERIALS

The following table shows the environmental benefits from using recycled materials as opposed to virgin resources:

BENEFIT	ALUMINIUM	STEEL	PAPER	GLASS
Reduced energy	90-97%	47-74%	23-74%	4-32%
Reduced air pollution	95%	85%	74%	20%
Reduced water pollution	97%	76%	35%	
Reduced mining wastes		97%		80%
Reduced water use		40%	58%	50%

programs include milk bottle tops, pull tabs and aluminium foil and trays. Rinse first.

◇ **Car oil:** Collect waste oil in the container it came in or use something similar. Many service stations collect this for recycling.

◇ **Car tyres:** If you aren't going to use your worn-out tyres for anything else – like a swing in the garden or a planter – the tyre fitting centre may take them for recycling.

◇ **Plastics:** Except for PET bottles (distinctive for their black bases), plastic currently has very little recycling potential so it's important to reuse plastics as much as possible. Stay informed about any new developments through your local councils.

WHERE TO NOW?

Once you've collected and sorted out different kinds of rubbish for recycling, it's time for the next step.

◇ **Local recyclers and bottle merchants.** You'll find address and phone details in your local telephone book.

◇ Most **local councils** have recycling schemes, at least for paper and glass – phone now for details. Bottle banks are another constructive move. If your local council isn't currently participating in collection for recycling, find out why not and lobby for change.

◇ **Your favourite charity or local hospital** is likely to have organised collection depots for any donations.

FACT

◇ 15 mature trees make 1 tonne of paper.
◇ Recycling half the paper used in the world today would save 8 million hectares of forest.

❖ PLASTICS ❖

Large amounts of energy, water and oil are required in the production of plastics. It's ironic that so many precious resources go into making a virtually indestructible article that is only used briefly – sometimes for no more than a few moments.

GUIDELINES

Avoid disposable items made from plastic whenever possible. Although currently plastic is not recycled on a large scale, the future is looking a little more promising with pilot programs for recycling domestic plastics being established around the world.

In the meantime the only thing you can do is cut down on the amount of waste plastic you produce. Following are a few suggestions on how you can do this.

◇ **Avoid buying meat and vegetables prepackaged in plastic** and displayed on styrofoam trays. If your supermarket or local shops don't offer unpackaged goods, voice your opinion and shop elsewhere until they change.

◇ **Take your own bag** or trolley when you go shopping to avoid accumulating more plastic carry bags. If you don't manage to avoid plastic bags completely, at least ensure you maximise their life by reusing them.

◇ **Avoid using plastic bags** and plastic cling wraps in the kitchen. A plate on top of a bowl of leftovers in the fridge does the same job as plastic wrap, or buy a set of storage containers and jars that can be reused for years to come.

◇ **Buy 100 per cent recyclable** alternatives to goods packaged in plastic.

◇ **Avoid man-made fibres** in clothing – choose leather over plastic for footwear.

◇ Avoid **disposable plates**, cups and food utensils.

◇ Don't buy **disposable razors** – buy a good razor that relies on disposable blades only.

◇ **Invest in a good pen** that will last for years and only require refills, or buy a fountain pen. Millions of plastic pens are thrown out every year.

◇ Buy **margarine and butter in paper wrappers** and transfer to a butter dish. Think about the number of plastic margarine tubs you threw out over the last 12 months. It's frightening when you consider that every other household did the same.

◇ Buy **soft drink in glass bottles**, preferably reusable.

◇ **Line your kitchen bin with newspaper** rather than plastic bin liners.

SOLAR BAGS

Some supermarket chains have now introduced the 'solar bag', a plastic carry bag that degrades in sunlight. Although this is a step in the right direction, it's not the answer.

Unfortunately, as the name 'solar bag' suggests, these bags require sunlight to degrade. When your rubbish is taken to the tip it's generally buried under more rubbish very quickly. Once solar bags are buried and away from direct sunlight, they won't break down.

If you end up with a collection of these bags, reuse them until they are completely worn out, then hang them on your washing line or somewhere in the sun till they degrade.

❖ MIXED ITEMS ❖

A mixed item is made from several different materials.

A mixed item with a metal base and a plastic applicator (like most aerosol spray cans), or a cardboard container with plastic lining, has little or no recycling potential. So far an economically viable process for separating all the different substances hasn't been developed. Keep this in mind when you are out shopping and look for recyclable alternatives.

Plastic Cap

Metal Base

FACT

Developed countries could reduce demand for paper pulp by at least one quarter through recycling. During World War 2, most Northern Hemisphere countries recovered and reused up to half their paper.

❖ ONE-WAY CONTAINERS ❖

Aluminium is the most energy-intensive commodity in common use. It wasn't until 1820 that scientists could refine it.
It's first use was as a toy rattle for Napoleon's son and at that time it was more precious and expensive than gold!

Carbonated beverage containers account for more than 5 per cent of household garbage in the USA. These containers are a major waste problem worldwide. This could be easily remedied by bringing back the returnable deposit system, whereby a cash deposit is refunded when the empty container is returned.

In South Australia, where a system of refundable deposits on drink cans is in place, they have an incredible 93 per cent return rate.

New York instigated a program requiring deposits on soft drink and beer containers. A study by the Beer Wholesalers Association showed that within 2 years of its implementation the New York deposit law had saved $US50 million in cleanup expenditures, $19 million on solid waste disposal and $50-$100 million on energy costs. Employment increased by at least 3,800 jobs.

More importantly, it was found that a deposit system encouraged people to conserve and recycle generally. Recycling of paper, scrap metal, oil and other materials increased in areas where a deposit system for bottles had been introduced.

The Environmental Protection Agency in the USA estimates that if compulsory returnable drink container legislation was enforced 500,000 tons of aluminium, 1.5 million tons of steel, 5.2 million tons of glass and 46 million barrels of oil would be saved annually in their country alone.

THE STORY OF ALUMINIUM

The first aluminium beverage can appeared on the market in 1963. In that year 11.5 billion cans were used in the USA of which 11.4 billion were made from steel. By 1985, the trend had completely reversed and aluminium cans accounted for 66 billion of the 70 billion used – a 94 per cent market share.

Until 1975, refillable glass bottles dominated the international beverage container markets. By 1981, the ratio in the USA reversed and most carbonated beverages were sold in one-way containers.

By 1985, aluminium cans and plastic bottles had achieved a 69 per cent share of the market volume, while refillable glass retained only a 16 per cent share.

WHAT YOU CAN DO

◇ Return all your **aluminium cans** for recycling.

◇ Why not **write to beer and soft drink companies** and let them know you prefer drinks in returnable, refundable glass bottles?

◇ Buy your milk in **returnable glass bottles** – milk cartons can't be recycled. Neighbourhood stores generally stock milk in glass bottles.

OLD CLOTHES

Old clothes not destined for the bazaar or for charity can go to recycling mills to be made into second-hand clothing (especially cotton and wool), flocking (for stuffing furniture and mattresses in place of feathers) and industrial cleaning cloths. Some recycled fabric is used in the hat-making trade. Rag merchants can use leathers, plastics, mixed fibres and cottons.

OLD COMPUTERS NEVER DIE

◇ Does your computer take a floppy disk? There are many excellent interactive educational disks on the market. Why not transform your old PC or Macintosh into your child's interactive learning centre?

◇ For the handyperson who is prepared to do some homework and likes to play with gadgets: If your computer has an in-built clock and an outlet then you can probably transform your computer into an elaborate switching device which could be used to control a simple robot or switch outside and inside lights on and off at random for security purposes at night. Look in the telephone book for a computer peripherals section for switching devices.

MENU

☐ BASIC MATHS
☐ WHERE IN THE WORLD IS CARMEN MIRANDA?
☐ LIGHTS AND POWER TIMING SWITCH
☐ LETTERS TO MANUFACTURERS
☐ RECYCLING DATABASE

SAVE ENERGY

- ❖ **Fossil fuels**
- ❖ **Energy alternatives**
- ❖ **An energy-efficient home**
- ❖ **The ozone story**
- ❖ **Heating**
- ❖ **The Greenhouse Effect**
- ❖ **Cooling**
- ❖ **Lighting**
- ❖ **Kitchen**
- ❖ **Acid rain**
- ❖ **Laundry**

Our energy habits are leading us to disaster. Scientists now know that coal, oil and natural gas – which supply us with about four-fifths of our global energy – are major causes of ozone depletion, contributing to both the Greenhouse Effect and acid rain.

> **FACT**
>
> The energy needed for a light bulb to shine for 10 hours, or a one-bar electric heater for 1 hour, releases about 2 kg of carbon dioxide into the atmosphere.

❖ IT'S EASY TO SAVE ENERGY ❖

Energy conservation is probably the easiest step to take in home ecology because you can see the effects almost immediately. The lower your energy bill, the better you are doing.

The average family wastes more energy than it actually uses. Reducing your energy use is just a matter of changing habits, for example, switch off the lights when you leave a room, close the door behind you or turn off the TV if no-one is watching it.

This section is full of energy-saving ideas and tips to help you run a more energy-efficient home.

FOSSIL FUELS

Energy is vital for many of our basic needs like transport, heating and food preparation. We rely heavily on burning fossil fuels to create this energy – this in turn has an enormous influence on our environment.

Coal

Coal is the most plentiful fossil fuel and is also the most polluting when burned. Carbon dioxide emissions from the combustion of coal are increasing the carbon dioxide content of the atmosphere and threatening to cause climatic changes through the Greenhouse Effect.

Emissions of sulphur dioxide and oxides of nitrogen from coal-fired power stations are involved in the production of acid rain. An estimated 100 million tonnes of

10 GOLDEN RULES

- ◆ **Insulate your home**
- ◆ **Install a solar system**
- ◆ **Heat only the rooms you use**
- ◆ **Wear more clothing instead of turning up the heat**
- ◆ **Switch off lights in areas not being used**
- ◆ **Ensure your oven and fridge seal properly**
- ◆ **Choose energy-efficient appliances**
- ◆ **Turn everything off when you go on holidays**
- ◆ **Keep doors to heated rooms closed**
- ◆ **Plug up draughts**

sulphur dioxide are released annually into the atmosphere.

This pollution could be reduced by washing and crushing the coal before it is burnt. Although some coal is washed, there is a general resistance because of the added expense.

Mining for coal can severely degrade the land and mining wastes poison the environment. Added to this is the risk to aquatic life through waterborne pollution.

Oil

It is estimated that the world's current oil reserves will be depleted in about 30 years. There is probably another 30 years' supply in as yet undiscovered oil resources. No matter how you look at it, time is running out and costs will soar as oil becomes increasingly scarce.

Over 2.5 billion tonnes of oil are consumed around the world annually. More than 3 million tonnes of this is discharged into the ocean, either through accidental spillage or the washing of tanks. This can cause enormous losses to all forms of marine life including birds, fish and plankton.

Oil is refined to separate the crude oil into different grades. This process causes both air and water pollution – 200,000 tonnes of oil pollute our oceans annually through seepage and accidental loss from refineries.

Gas

Natural gas is the cleanest of all the fossil fuels. Unfortunately this resource is unevenly distributed – the difficulty of transporting gas makes it a viable option for only a few countries. Burning gas still creates a certain amount of air pollution and laying pipelines can be destructive to habitats and wildlife.

SOLAR HEATING

Passive solar heating: You need large expanses of glass facing the sun. Replace roof tiles with special glass panels. The temperature inside rises higher than the outside as the glass lets in sunlight which becomes trapped inside as heat.

Active solar heating: Install a flat plate collector which absorbs the heat and heats water circulating inside the plate. Once the water is heated, it can be stored in a tank for on-tap hot water, or you can use it to supplement an existing hot water supply.

❖ ALTERNATIVES ❖

With non-renewable, polluting energy sources like fossil fuel dwindling, it's time to invest in renewable, clean energy sources.

SOLAR POWER

Solar power is the least polluting form of energy you can use in the home. Although only .01 per cent of global energy is currently solar, there has been a massive investment in solar technology in recent years.

The world's largest solar plant is The Solar One in California. It provides the energy needs of around 2,000 homes. The future of solar energy is looking brighter although in some countries, like the UK, only co-generation systems may be feasible.

WIND POWER

Wind power is another source of clean power. There are many successful examples of the use of wind to produce energy. In the USA over 10,000 windmills generate as much electricity as a conventional power station. California anticipates that one fifth of its electricity will be produced by wind power by the end of the century. In Denmark, 16 windmills now supply one tenth of the electricity supplied to 4,000 residents.

OCEAN, GEOTHERMAL AND HYDROPOWER

These are other potential sources of energy for the future.

HOUSEHOLD ENERGY USE	
Home heating	50%
Hot water	27%
Lighting and small appliances	13%
Cooking	10%

❖ AN ENERGY-EFFICIENT HOME ❖

When you set out to buy a new home there are many factors to take into consideration – the neighbourhood, convenience to public transport, proximity to schools, shopping and recreational facilities.

HOW DOES YOUR HOME RATE?
Checklist

☐ Is the house situated to make the most of the winter sun?
☐ Is it properly insulated?
☐ What type of hot water system does it have and has it been well maintained?
☐ Will the windows give you good summer ventilation?
☐ Do the landscaping features offer you protection from, or take advantage of, the elements?
☐ Does the house have an existing solar system? Would you need to do major renovations to install one?
☐ Does the material in its construction suit the climate?

All of these points are well worth checking. Energy saved will benefit your purse as well as the environment.

BUILDING A HOME

If you are building your own home there is no better time to get it right energy wise. Planning for energy conservation early on in the construction stage may mean no extra cost.

Let your architect know energy efficiency is an important design consideration. If you are buying a project home, look at the plans critically.

Checklist

☐ Properly insulated walls and ceilings and lofts.
☐ Verandahs for protective external shading and a useful outdoor living space.
☐ Building materials that suit the climate.
☐ Skylights to improve natural light.
☐ Windows that let the winter sun in and keep the summer sun out. If you do want windows on the side of the house that faces the summer sun they should be as small as possible and be either fixed with external blinds or shaded by nearby buildings, trees or shrubs. Arrange windows to maximise ventilation in summer. Avoid aluminium windows and roofing. Vast amounts of energy are used to produce aluminium; rainforests are cleared to mine the bauxite needed.
☐ Double-glazed windows and doors
☐ Weather-stripped doors and windows.
☐ Plantation grown timber (not rainforest timbers) for building and furniture.
☐ Floor coverings to suit the climate – carpets for cool climates, tile or wooden floors for warm climates.
☐ A solar hot water system inside – external hot water systems often suffer greater heat loss. The hot water system should be as close to the kitchen and main bathroom as possible to reduce the time it takes for hot water to flow through long pipes.

YOUR EXISTING HOME

There are several ways you can make your existing home more energy-efficient. Even though these changes will cost you money initially, many of them will pay for themselves over and over again as energy costs continue to rise.

The Earth is surrounded by a thin layer of gas known as the ozone layer, which lies in the stratosphere about 20-25 km above the Earth's surface. The ozone layer protects us from the sun's harmful radiation by filtering out ultraviolet (UV) radiation and, in particular, by providing a protective screen against harmful UV-B radiation, which increases the incidence of certain kinds of skin cancer.

The ozone layer is being disturbed by long-lived pollutants. Chlorofluorocarbons (CFCs) and nitrogen oxides are responsible for ozone depletion, while methane affects ozone levels in other ways.

The continued depletion of the ozone layer is likely to increase health hazards like skin cancer and eye cataracts, and will also affect the production of food and timber.

CFCs are used in air conditioners, refrigerators, dry cleaning, pressure-pack cans and in the production of plastic foams – the material takeaway food is packaged in.

The threat to the ozone layer is a major environmental problem and will remain so until significant action is taken to control releases of CFCs, nitrogen oxides and methane. You can start now by not buying products which contain or use these pollutants, and by reducing the amount of fuel you use.

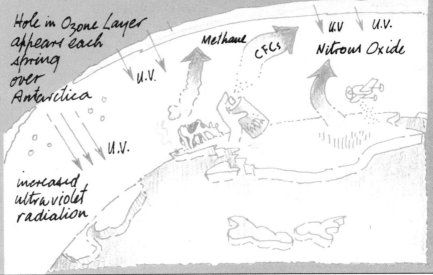

Hole in Ozone Layer appears each spring over Antarctica

increased ultra violet radiation

U.V.

U.V.

Methane

CFCs

U.V U.V.

Nitrous Oxide

Checklist

☐ Install a solar hot water system.

☐ Weather strip your doors and windows.

☐ Insulate your home. Heat rises and escapes out the top of the house and the summer sun beats down on it. Make it a priority to insulate your roof. Ideally, the outer walls should be insulated as well but this can be expensive.

☐ Attach awnings to shade from the summer sun.

☐ Landscape for energy conservation. Plant windbreaks to obstruct the prevailing cold winds, plant deciduous trees that will allow the winter sun through but block the harsh summer sun.

❖ HEATING ❖

Plugging draughts can save you up to 20 per cent of your annual heating bill as well as adding to your general comfort.

◇ **Your first task** is to assess how well your rooms retain heat. Heating a draughty room will prove expensive and ineffective.

◇ **Weather stripping** is one of the most efficient ways to eliminate draughts. If you stand inside your closed window on a breezy day and still feel a draught then you need to weather strip. A variety of cheap, easy-to-install weather-stripping options are available from your local hardware store.

◇ The best way to **isolate draughts** is to close all your windows and doors, light a stick of incense or a candle and walk around your home. The smoke trail or flickering candle will be a good guide to where your trouble spots are.

◇ **Insulate the roof.** Up to 35 per cent of heat loss or gain is through the ceiling.

◇ **Double-glazed windows** can save up to 30 per cent on your heating bill.

◇ **Snake-shaped bolsters** are an easy, cheap way to prevent draughts from under doors. These are very simple to make, even without a sewing machine.

◇ **Curtains cut down draughts** from windows – the longer they are, the more effective they'll be. Choose light colours that reflect both heat and light and use thermal-backed lining fabric. Clean windows will let more sun into rooms on sunny winter days so keep the curtains open. On cloudy days or at night, close the curtains to avoid heat loss.

◇ **An unused fireplace** can be a major source of draughts. If you don't use it, install an efficient combustion stove, brick it up or block it.

YOUR HOT WATER SYSTEM

◇ **Use cold water** when filling jugs or rinsing hands. Most people don't even wait for the water to run hot – it's just a habit.

◇ **Turn off the hot water system** when you go on holiday or leave the house vacant.

◇ **Turn the thermostat setting down** on your hot water system – there's no need to have scalding water straight from the tap. If you consistently have to add cold water, the temperature is set too high. Around 60°C is adequate.

◇ **Insulate** your hot water system.

◇ **Install aerators** and water-efficient shower heads. These use up to five times less water but there is no noticeable reduction in pressure.

◇ **Try to wash up only once** a day or only when the dishwasher is full.

◇ **Take showers** instead of baths.

◇ **Repair a dripping hot water tap** as soon as you notice. It can waste about ten bathtubs of hot water a month.

◇ **Install a solar hot water system** when it is time to replace your old system. Although the initial cost will be higher, your continued fuel saving will soon pay dividends.

MAKING THE MOST OF HEAT

◇ Try to **keep doors to heated rooms closed**. When you do leave the room, shut the door

behind you and try to do everything in one trip instead of coming and going every 5 minutes.

◇ Remember, heat rises. If you live in **a two-storey home**, have your living areas upstairs.

◇ **Only heat the rooms you are using** and keep the doors of unused rooms closed.

◇ **Put on extra clothes** rather than turning up the heat.

◇ If you have **central heating**, don't set the thermostat too high. Turn it down a few degrees at a time – you'll hardly notice the difference.

◇ Put **a woollen blanket** under your sheets for extra warmth. Thick cotton flannel sheets are snug and inviting on cold nights.

◇ When you have finished your bath, let the **hot water** continue to heat the bathroom. Only drain it away when the water has turned cold.

THE GREENHOUSE EFFECT

Carbon dioxide (CO_2) regulates the amount of heat the Earth absorbs from the sun. About half of the carbon dioxide released is absorbed by oceans, forests and the process of limestone deposition. The rest collects in the atmosphere. Trees use CO_2 for their own growth and are our main natural defence against excessively high levels of carbon dioxide. The more trees we cut down, the less protection we have. Apart from CO_2 atmospheric levels of CFCs and methane are also on the increase. These 'Greenhouse gases' are warming the atmosphere by trapping the heat radiated back into it from the Earth's surface.

It is estimated that within the next 100 years the temperature of the Earth could rise by 2-3°C. This average increase would be unevenly distributed, ranging from perhaps less than a degree at the equator to up to 6°C at higher latitudes. As the temperature rises, so too will sea

levels, not good news for the half of the world's population who live in coastal areas.

The Greenhouse Effect can be lessened if we learn to conserve energy better, and invest now in developing and using energy sources which don't pollute the atmosphere.

❖ COOLING ❖

◇ **Open windows** to encourage cooling breezes.

◇ **Good insulation** reduces heat entering your home from outside.

◇ **Light-coloured exterior walls** reflect sunlight and heat.

◇ **Plant trees** around the home for shade. Deciduous trees provide shade in summer and allow the sunlight in when they shed their leaves in winter.

◇ **Use air conditioners sparingly** as they use CFCs. If you do use an air conditioner it need never be set lower than 25°C. Check and clean your filters regularly as the fans have to work much harder when the filters are dirty. Better still, use a ceiling fan.

❖ LIGHTING ❖

The energy output of conventional incandescent light bulbs is approximately 90 per cent heat and only 10 per cent light. They are the least efficient artificial light source available.

The wattage of a globe refers to the energy used not the light emitted. For example, a 100 watt globe only gives 50 per cent more light than four 25 watt globes.

◇ **Buy globes to suit your needs** only. Bright lights are not really necessary in most areas of the home – reduce where you can but don't go to extremes. Always have enough light for safety and to avoid eye strain.

◇ **Keep your light bulbs clean** – dirty bulbs can reduce lighting efficiency by up to 50 per cent.

◇ **Light-coloured walls** reduce the amount of light needed in a room.

◇ **Fit dimmers to light switches** – they reduce the amount of electricity used.

◇ **Use fluorescent tubes.** They are about four times more efficient than incandescent bulbs and will last at least five times longer. The circular or U-shaped tubes are a little more efficient than the straight variety. The new, thinner fluorescent tubes use around 10 per cent less energy again.

◇ Although **fluorescent lights** are more expensive initially they will last 5-10 times longer than an incandescent bulb and only use around one quarter of the energy. When first switched on they consume the energy equivalent of 20 minutes running time. Use them in places like the kitchen where lights stay on for longer. Fluorescent bulbs that fit into ordinary sockets are now available. You may have to buy them through specialist lighting stores, but they are worth searching for.

◇ **Only light rooms you are actually occupying** – when you leave a room get into the habit of switching the light off.

◇ For maximum light efficiency, **place lamps in the corner of the room** to take advantage of two walls to reflect light.

❖ KITCHEN ❖

Following our general tips, you can even change the way you boil water to save energy.

GENERAL TIPS

◇ **Use all household appliances sparingly.** It takes 5-6 tonnes of coal to provide the electricity for a fully-equipped kitchen annually.

◇ **Microwave ovens** use considerably less energy than conventional ovens. Fan-forced or convection ovens ensure more efficient hot air distribution, giving better cooking results and reduced energy consumption.

◇ If possible **turn off your gas pilot** – the wasted gas can account for up to 15 per cent of your gas bill. When it's time to purchase a new gas cooker, buy one without a pilot light.

◇ **Check that your oven door is sealing properly** by shutting a piece of paper in it. The door should hold it in place. Open the oven as little as possible when you are cooking.

◇ **Keep stoves clean** to

MODERN HOUSEWORK
Even with all of the modern, so-called labour-saving devices, US research indicates that American women spend more time on housework now than they did 20 years ago! One of the reasons for this is that houses tend to be larger and more sophisticated in design.

maximise reflective heat.

◇ **Defrost your food prior to cooking** – it is safer and more energy efficient.

◇ **Turn the stove off** a few minutes before food is cooked. There will be sufficient heat left to finish the job. Once you've

ACID RAIN

Acid rain is fallout from industrial pollutants, sometimes as acidified natural rain and sometimes in the form of dry deposits. Most of the pollutants are caused by burning fossil fuels. A significant number also come from vehicle exhausts. Acid rain damages forests, plants, and crops, acidifies lakes, rivers and groundwater, and corrodes building materials.

Acid rain can fall great distances from its point of origin. Although until recently the problem was confined to the Northern Hemisphere, there are now signs of its effects being found in Australia and Brazil.

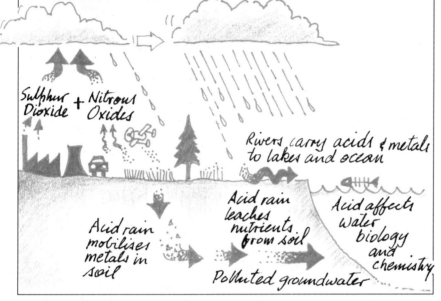

Sulphur Dioxide + Nitrous Oxides

Rivers carry acids & metals to lakes and ocean

Acid rain mobilises metals in soil

Acid rain leaches nutrients from soil

Acid affects water biology and chemistry

Polluted groundwater

brought a pan of water to the boil, turn the stove right down – it will maintain its temperature.

◇ **When boiling water** only use as much as you need to cover the food – better still use a pressure cooker or steamer. Pressure cookers drastically cut down cooking time – a real bonus for busy cooks as well as an energy saver.

◇ **Put lids on saucepans** – this will reduce cooking time needed.

◇ **The smaller you cut your vegetables**, the faster they'll cook.

◇ **Avoid using aluminium foil** when cooking. If you do use it put the dull side outermost, and then recycle it!

◇ **Cook more than one dish** at a time.

COOKING UTENSILS

Your cooking utensils are an important part of energy efficiency.

◇ **Baking tins** should be a thin metal and dark in colour to encourage transfer of heat to the food inside them.

◇ Avoid using **baking tins with lids** – this forms an insulating pocket of air above the food which in turn slows down heat transfer.

◇ **Pots and pans** should have flat, thick bottoms and be as close to the size of the elements as possible, if not larger.

◇ **The sides of pots** should be vertical to reduce heat loss from the walls.

◇ Make sure **saucepan lids** fit tightly.

APPLIANCES

◇ **Small electric appliances** like frypans, slow cookers or deep fryers use considerably less energy than ovens.

◇ **Choose an appliance to suit the job** – if you are making toast, use the toaster not the grill. If the job is small, use a small appliance.

◇ Avoid kettles designed to sit on the stove top. **Electric kettles** are much more efficient as the first thing they heat is the actual water.

◇ Use **an automatic switch-off kettle** or jug and only heat as much water as you actually need. There are new, fast-boil appliances on the market that allow you to boil as little as one cupful at a time.

◇ Select a kettle that has its element at the bottom rather than half-way up – this will allow you to **boil smaller amounts of water**.

◇ Buy **energy-efficient appliances** and always buy the best you can afford – they'll last much longer.

◇ **Choose metal** over plastic.

◇ **Don't buy unnecessary gadgets**, they're often designed more for a gimmick than practical use.

REFRIGERATORS AND FREEZERS

Refrigerators and freezers run 24 hours a day, so assess your needs carefully and buy one that fits the bill. Why pay to cool space that isn't used? Compare the energy use of different machines – if you are unsure, ask the sales person for advice. Buy a well-insulated, energy-efficient unit.

◇ Put your refrigerator in the coolest part of the kitchen – never in direct sunlight. **Avoid over-cooling your fridge.** Adjust the thermostat until you find the suitable temperature.

◇ **Manually defrost** your fridge regularly – an automatic defroster is often more convenient but uses more energy. Ensure all the doors seal properly.

◇ **Defrost food slowly** and safely by moving it from the freezer to the refrigerator section.

◇ Some **two-door freezer/ refrigerators** have independent switches for each compartment. This is very handy when you go away on holiday as you can turn off the fresh food section without affecting frozen foods. Two-door fridge models with the freezer below are more energy efficient than those with the freezer on top. The side-by-side types are the least efficient of all.

◇ **Fancy extras** are very nice to have but use more energy. Heated butter compartments, water dispensers and ice makers all add to running costs.

◇ If you need **a separate freezer**, buy a chest model with a lid that lifts up. Cold air falls out of the upright models whenever you open the door. It's estimated that upright models use a third more energy.

◇ If your fridge door doesn't swing back and snap shut, slightly raise the front and let gravity do the rest. **An open fridge door** will increase the power bill and ruin your food.

◇ Turn off and **empty your fridge** when you are going away. Leave the door ajar.

◇ **Organise food for convenience** – keep the items you use regularly within easy reach. This will minimise the time you stand with the door open.

◇ Only put things in the fridge that need to be kept cool. Items like **honey and peanut butter** can be kept in the pantry.

◇ Never put hot food directly into the fridge. **Allow food to cool first.**

DISHWASHERS

◇ Use dishwashers only when you have a **full load**.

◇ Always use **biodegradable detergents** and only in moderation.

◇ **Switch your machine off** when it gets to the 'dry cycle'. Just open the door and pull the trays out – the plates are generally hot enough to dry almost instantly.

❖ LAUNDRY ❖

There are many easy ways to save energy in your laundry.

WASHING MACHINES

When you buy a new washing machine, seek out an energy-efficient model. Some washing machines use up to four times more energy than others to do the same job.

◇ As with all your household appliances, **buy a good quality machine** and maintain it properly. A front-end loading machine is the best choice for energy saving – it uses 24 per cent less total water, 40 per cent less hot water and 46 per cent less energy than top loaders with a similar load capacity.

◇ Look for a machine with **different settings and cycles** so that you can do a short cycle for the not-so-dirty clothes, or use the machine only half full for a small, urgent wash.

◇ **Wait till you have a full load** of washing before using the machine.

◇ **Avoid overloading** either your washer or your dryer.

◇ **Use cold water** whenever possible. Always use cold water on the rinse cycle (the temperature of the rinse water doesn't affect the cleaning).

DRYERS

Clothes dryers use lots of energy. Dry your clothes in the sun whenever the weather permits. This will reduce your electricity bills and preserve your clothes.

◇ If you have a **timer switch** on your dryer, be realistic when setting it. Experiment to see how long different types of loads need for drying.

◇ **Variable temperature settings** – should be used to increase energy efficiency. If you have a load of delicates to dry, only use the cool setting.

◇ Buy a dryer with **good insulation** in the outer metal box to reduce noise and heat loss.

◇ Separate, **free-standing dryers** use less energy than washing machines with built-in tumble dryers.

◇ When you dry more than one load, **do loads consecutively** to avoid heating the unit up from scratch.

◇ **Cut down on ironing time** and energy by hanging your clothes on the washing line and folding them as you take them down. Iron a load in one session, rather than one item at a time.

SAVE FUEL

- ❖ **Fuel**
- ❖ **Goods transportation**
- ❖ **Noise pollution**
- ❖ **How to cut down**
- ❖ **Driving**
- ❖ **Car care**
- ❖ **Buying a car**
- ❖ **Alternatives**
- ❖ **Lead-free petrol**

Lobby your local council for improved traffic planning – it's important to divert traffic out of residential areas and onto major roads as well as reducing the overall amount of traffic.

FACT

◇ There are about 600 million vehicles in use worldwide – twice as many as 10 years ago. Another 30 million are manufactured annually and this is increasing.

◇ The average car takes the energy equivalent of 1500 litres of oil to manufacture and uses at least 10,000 litres of fuel before it is scrapped or dumped.

❖ UNDREAMT-OF MOBILITY ❖

Cars have changed our lives by giving us undreamt-of mobility. Today we think nothing of travelling 50-100 kilometres to work everyday, when less than a century ago many people didn't venture that far in a lifetime.

Everything has its price. Motor vehicles are a major cause of air pollution. They emit unburnt hydrocarbons, carbon monoxide, oxides of nitrogen and lead into the atmosphere to create acid rain and photochemical smog.

Modern cities and towns have been shaped by wheels to the extent that one third of the land in an average city is taken up by carparks and roads. Outside cities, freeways and other major roads consume even larger areas. Smaller roads are a problem when they go through environmentally sensitive areas.

This section has lots of tips on how you can reduce the amount of air pollution you cause, save fuel and be more aware of the environment.

FUEL
Despite tighter environmental regulations to cut down on car emissions and improvements in fuel economy, more people now own and use cars, and the volume of pollutants produced has also risen. It's time to invest in clean, renewable energy sources such as solar, electric and hydrogen-powered transport.

10 GOLDEN RULES

◆ **Use public transport whenever convenient**
◆ **Buy locally produced and packaged goods**
◆ **Adopt fuel-saving driving techniques**
◆ **Cut down on car trips**
◆ **Avoid energy-consuming extras on your car**
◆ **Buy a small, lightweight car that runs on lead-free petrol**
◆ **Car pool with fellow commuters**
◆ **Walk if you only have a short distance to travel**
◆ **Shop locally**
◆ **Keep your car properly maintained**

NOISE POLLUTION

Don't add to noise pollution levels unnecessarily.

◇ Horns should only be used to alert another person to possible danger – not just because you've had a bad day!

◇ Car alarms are a necessity today but their late-night sirens can be particularly annoying to neighbours. Buy an alarm that won't go off if a leaf falls on the car.

◇ Unnecessary engine revving and tyre screeching adds to the noise level – especially for people who live on a busy street or near an intersection.

◇ Late night or early morning slamming of doors will cause unnecessary wear and tear to your vehicle as well as grumpy neighbours!

GOODS TRANSPORTATION

Every item you buy from the supermarket, every appliance, book, beer, pen and so on has been transported from where it was produced and packaged to the point of sale. Goods often travel thousands of kilometres to reach their destination.

Most food used to be produced by the community for the community. Once commercial growers began to specialise, large amounts of one crop were grown to supply both local and export markets. Today there are massive wheat belts, dairying areas and fruit-growing regions across the world.

Many countries have centralised their processing and distribution operations in major cities. Food is grown in the country, taken to the city to be processed and packaged, then transported back to the country for sale.

This system is a drain on fuel resources and adds to our pollution problems. Always make it a priority to buy locally produced and packaged goods. Check the label before you buy.

FACT

Each year more than **450,000** tonnes of lead are released into the air. More than half of this is from cars.

❖ HOW TO CUT DOWN ❖

Before you look at how you can cut down on fuel, try to gauge how often you use your car.

◇ Keep **a diary** of your car trips – where you went, distance travelled, how many passengers, and weather conditions. Work out where you can cut down. Set yourself an easy target and try to eliminate at least one trip a week.

◇ When the weather is fine, and your intended trip is less than a 20 minute walk, why not **get some exercise** and walk instead?

◇ Do you really need two cars? If one of them sits parked outside work each day, why not **join a car pool** or use public transport?

◇ **Public transport** is a very convenient form of travelling and needs your support to run efficiently. No parking, no waiting at lights or sitting in traffic jams. A bus or train ride can also be therapeutic, providing a much-needed opportunity to sit and think, nap, read a book or simply watch the world go by.

◇ If you pick up the children every afternoon from school, and see other parents from your street doing the same, approach them about **taking turns**. Why send three cars to the same destination when one can do the job?

DRIVING
The way you drive can significantly reduce fuel consumption and pollution.

◇ Drive a car that uses **lead-free petrol**. Remember, diesel fuel has no lead emissions.

◇ **Slow down and save petrol.** Consumption increases with speed. A speed reduction from 100kph to 80kph can result in a 25 per cent reduction in fuel.

◇ **Electronic ignition** saves fuel.

◇ **Avoid peak hour traffic** when possible (as if you don't already!) – more fuel is consumed in stop/start traffic.

◇ **Think ahead** when you drive. When approaching your turn move into the appropriate lane in plenty of time.

◇ **Don't push each gear to the limit.**

◇ **Switch off** the engine when stuck in a traffic jam. There's no need to keep the car idling.

◇ The more weight in the car, the more fuel you use. Check that you are not carrying **unnecessary loads** in your boot.

◇ **Don't overfill your petrol tank** – it'll only be lost through the overflow pipe.

◇ **Remove roof racks** if you are not using them. Any fitted extras that affect the aerodynamics of your car increase fuel consumption.

◇ **Inflate your tyres** to the correct pressure to reduce both petrol consumption and wear on tyres.

◇ **Drive smoothly**, accelerate gently and avoid panic breaking. This reduces fuel consumption, and saves unnecessary wear and tear on your car.

◇ **Don't drive with your foot on the brake**. You use more fuel and create unnecessary stress on your vehicle.

◇ **Don't overuse your choke**. As soon as the car is running smoothly, release the choke.

◇ Be courteous when driving. **Slow down in residential areas** and near schools. Don't race your engine impatiently at pedestrian crossings or traffic lights.

◇ Don't let other drivers bully you into going faster. **Choose your own speed** and stick to it.

◇ Be aware of **pedestrians, cyclists and wildlife** – always anticipate their presence on the road.

ADDED EXTRAS
Many of the features put on cars today are gimmicks only – they increase fuel consumption and add to atmospheric pollution. Choose small, simple cars without the energy-consuming extras.

◇ Automotive air conditioning increases fuel consumption by more than 10 per cent. It is also responsible for around 35% of CFC emissions.

◇ Automotive transmissions use around 10 per cent more fuel than manual gears, particularly in heavy traffic conditions.

◇ Roof racks, bull bars, sun visors or any attachment that is fitted to the exterior of your car will increase fuel consumption due to increased air friction.

❖ CAR CARE ❖

Keep your car running smoothly by having a service and tune up twice a year. Get your pollution control devices checked at the same time.

◇ Keep **tyres** properly inflated.

◇ **Prevent rust** – this will extend the life of your vehicle.

◇ Fit an **electronic ignition** – this saves fuel.

◇ If your car is fitted with an air conditioner, use it only when necessary. **Air conditioners increase fuel consumption** and leak CFCs into the atmosphere. Have your hose and seals checked for leaks. If your air conditioner needs repair ask the service station to use CFC recovery equipment.

◇ If you do your own car maintainence, **dispose of any mess carefully**. Never put oil into drains. Keep oil in a container and drop it off for recycling.

CLEANING

◇ When you wash the car **don't leave the hose running**. Use a bucket for washing and use the hose for rinsing only.

◇ **Avoid toxic cleaners** for the car, pure soap and water will do the job. Use a simple wax polish.

> ### LITTER BAGS
> How often do you see people throwing litter from their cars? Always carry your own litter bag or box in the car. Bags can easily be suspended from the dashboard. Persuade your friends to do the same.

BUYING A CAR

When you're next in the market for a new car, assess your needs and choose a car that suits.

◇ **Buy a smaller, more energy-efficient car** with anti-pollution gear. Diesel cars are able to recover 33 per cent of the heat and energy released from the engine; petrol cars can only recover about 25 per cent.

◇ Buy a car that uses **lead-free petrol** and make sure it has

been rust-proofed and zinc-protected for longer body life.

◇ Some cars are painted using water-borne, rather than solvent-borne, **paints**. Better for the worker and the atmosphere.

◇ Support car manufacturers that have a proven record in manufacturing **environmentally sensitive cars**.

◇ Choose **a manual car** – it uses less fuel.

◇ **Avoid air conditioning** in your car. In Australia, 35 per cent of all CFC use is attributable to automobile air conditioning.

◇ Buy a **second-hand** car fitted with anti-pollution devices if possible. If not, check if after-market gear is available.

❖ ALTERNATIVES ❖

We have all become so used to the convenience of having a car that we overlook the more obvious ways to get from point A to point B.

PUBLIC TRANSPORT

Public transport is up to 60 times more fuel-efficient than travelling solo in your car. It is cheaper and often easier to catch a bus or a train or a tube, even though public transport does have its inadequacies. The best way you can help to support and improve the service is to use it.

If you rely on public transport as a regular means of travel but find the service inadequate, write to the relevant transport authority suggesting ways they could improve the service.

Find out how other people feel about the current service in your area and encourage them to write also. Leave petitions in local shops. Your collective voice does count with future planning.

Get a current timetable from your local services if it's a while since you used public transport. Also ask for information on reduced prices and concession tickets.

> ### FACT
> In the motor industry, many leading companies now recover the polyvinyl chloride in scraps of car-seat fabric by washing the material in a solvent. Previously, the scraps had been incinerated, causing vinyl chloride, a potent carcinogen, to be released into the atmosphere.

THE BICYCLE

Cycling is an enjoyable, efficient and convenient way to travel. A bicycle is non-polluting, cheap to maintain and helps to keep you healthy.

People should be encouraged to use bicycles more and the best way to do that is to improve safety standards. If your town or city is short on bicycle paths and lanes write to the local planning authorities and register concern. Get in touch with a bicycle club and enquire about campaigns related to safer cycling.

If the idea of cycling through city traffic is too daunting, why not become a weekend cyclist? Cycling is relaxing, lots of fun and great for sightseeing.

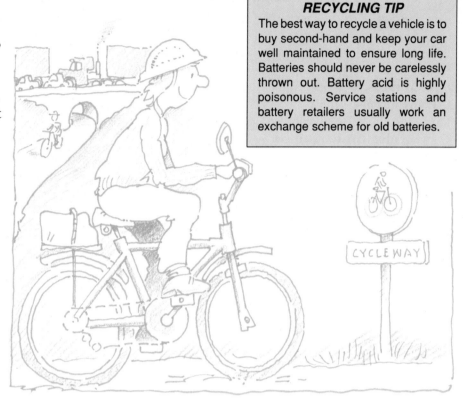

COMBUSTION POLLUTION

Cars produce five major forms of air pollution.

◇ **Hydrocarbons (HCs)**
These are largely responsible for the photochemical smogs that choke cities. and can cause breathing distress, asthma attacks and even help trigger heart failure. Road vehicles contribute 40% of hydrocarbon emissions in OECD (Organisation for Economic and Cooperative Development) countries.

◇ **Nitrogen oxides (NOx)**
Produced by all combustion processes, from power stations to motor scooters. These emissions are implicated in photochemical smogs and acid-rain problems.

◇ **Carbon monoxide (CO)**
The carbon monoxide in your car's exhaust emissions is very poisonous, and fatal in concentrated doses. Motor vehicles contribute about 75% of total CO emissions in OECD countries.

◇ **Particulates**
Road vehicles are a major source of black smoke and particulates (very fine particles, probably mostly of carbon) in urban areas. Black smoke affects visibility, blackens buildings and clothes and has been implicated in the onset of cancer and other diseases.

◇ **Lead**
Lead damages the brain and central nervous system. Lead is added to petrol so it is easy to eliminate.

WALKING

Walking is not only good for your health, it puts you in touch with your surroundings. Try leaving the car at home tomorrow. You'll be astounded at the things you never noticed before.

Walking gives you time to think and plan – a real bonus in today's busy world. Choose routes that have the least traffic. Take back streets and enjoy the peace.

LEAD-FREE PETROL

Lead has been linked with brain damage and nervous disorders, yet it is pumped into the atmosphere daily by motor vehicles. Find out how much it would cost to have your car converted for lead-free petrol. This involves having your car valves replaced with the harder type.

PROTECTING WILDLIFE

The building of motorways and roads, the constant clearing of virgin forests and the increasing urban sprawl have all taken their toll on wildlife. Habitat loss is one of the most pressing problems facing wildlife species worldwide as cities and transport networks expand in ever-widening circles.

Lead in the atmosphere from car emissions is harmful to wildlife. Airborne emissions spread the problem far afield (high lead concentrations are being diagnosed in places as remote as Greenland).

The daily death toll of animals run down on our roads and highways is a sad statistic.

You can help protect wildlife and their habitats by following some simple guidelines.

◇ Drive a car that uses lead-free petrol.
◇ Don't speed on open roads.
◇ Switch off your air conditioner when you don't need it.
◇ Ensure your car is fitted with efficient anti-pollution gear.
◇ Use your car less – walk, cycle and use public transport whenever possible.
◇ Always slow down in wildlife areas, especially where you see a sign indicating a common crossing point for wildlife.

◇ Always stop if you hit an animal to help in any way you can.
◇ Cut down on unnecessary trips.
◇ Do you really need a second car?
◇ Don't destroy wildlife habitats by cutting back hedgerows and clearing grass at the side of the road.
◇ Plant native trees in an effort to create new habitats for displaced species.

SAVE WATER

Fresh, clean water and plenty of it is something that can no longer be taken for granted.

FACT

Over 97 % of the world's water is salt. Of the remaining fresh water, very little is available to us – most of it is frozen in ice caps and glaciers or lies too far underground to get at easily.

Lakes and rivers, which are our traditional source of fresh water, contain only one hundredth of one per cent of the total surface water.

❖ FRESH, CLEAN WATER ❖

Good standards of water purity are something the whole community has to fight for. We must begin to conserve our precious water resources.

This section is full of tips on how you can save water and keep it clean in the home, at work and in your leisure activities.

WATER POLLUTION

Rivers, lakes and oceans have always been used as dumping grounds for waste. This includes sewage pumped directly into the ocean, domestic outfall from drains and highly toxic wastes from industry and agriculture. This waste has caused phenomenal damage to marine ecosystems, and made many of the beaches near cities and towns a potential health risk.

The ocean currents that bring sewage back to our beaches also circulates waste far beyond our back doors. High levels of DDT have been detected in Antarctic penguins, thousands of miles from its source.

Remember the basic code – **if in doubt, leave it out**. Most waste isn't suitable for disposal through the sewerage system.
◇ Never pour **cooking oil or fat** down the sink – it doesn't mix with water. Solidified fat can go on the compost or be put out with the garbage. Oil should be returned to its container and put out with the garbage, or buried in the garden away from plants.

10 GOLDEN RULES

- ◆ **Fix dripping taps promptly**
- ◆ **Choose phosphate-free detergent**
- ◆ **Use recycled, unbleached toilet paper**
- ◆ **Never dispose of toxic waste down the drain**
- ◆ **Shower instead of bathing**
- ◆ **Turn taps off properly**
- ◆ **Observe water bans**
- ◆ **Reuse washing water in the garden**
- ◆ **Water your garden in the early morning or early evening**
- ◆ **Don't do your laundry until you have a full load**

BOTTLED WATER

Bottled water of every kind has become big business. Some of the leading European brands are on sale all over the world.

The drain on energy resources to package and transport this cleaner-than-clean water is enormous.

Treat bottled water as the luxury it is. Buy a brand that is locally supplied and bottled in recyclable containers.

Why not try the local 'on tap' kind? There are many varieties of water filters available for home use. Some filter out more chemicals and pollutants than others. Shop around for one that best suits your needs.

◇ **Detergents** damage the environment, particularly those containing phosphates. Try using pure soap for washing clothes as well as dishes. If you do use detergents, use them sparingly and buy biodegradable brands only. If you use pure soap for washing up, the water can be used to water your garden afterwards.

◇ Keep your **toiletries** simple – pure soap and basic shampoos. Shop around for brands that don't have harmful additives. (Try some of our natural recipes throughout the book.)

◇ Avoid white or coloured **toilet paper** – they contain dyes and bleaches that are pollutants. Toilet paper marked 'suitable for septic tanks' is usually free of these, as is recycled toilet paper.

◇ Avoid **chemical cleaners** for your toilet. The flush toilet was specifically designed for hygiene without chemicals. The coloured variety are generally more cosmetic than cleansing. A loo brush and some vinegar will do the job just as well.

◇ Don't throw **coffee grounds and tea leaves** down the sink or toilet. Put them on your garden instead.

◇ Never pour **milk** down the sink – it's such a waste.

◇ **Disposable nappies** are a major waste problem. The billions that are sold and disposed of annually don't degrade. If you buy disposable nappies, put them in your bin for collection, never into the sewerage system. Why not try a nappy service? It works out cheaper and the door-to-door service will be a timesaver.

◇ **Sanitary towels** should be wrapped and put out with the garbage – never flush them down the toilet.

◇ **Condoms** should go into the garbage – never down the toilet.

◇ Wrap **leftover paint and turpentine** before putting it in your bin. Choose water-based paints over oil-based. Clean your brushes away from drains.

◇ Never put **toxic substances** like insecticides or kerosene down the drain.

◇ **Ashtrays** should never be emptied down the toilet and don't dispose of cigarette butts down the drain.

◇ Only use **non-toxic anti-fouling paint** on your boat to prevent encrustations. Toxic paints leach into the water and can have a devastating effect on marine life.

◇ Check your boat regularly to ensure it is not **leaking oil**.

◇ Don't **litter**. Take your rubbish home with you.

◇ If a company is a proven polluter, **don't buy** their products or use their services.

❖ SAVING WATER AT HOME ❖

Water is so easy to waste when it's on tap. Try to limit the amount of water you use. Here's our room-by-room look at thirsty rooms.

KITCHEN

◇ Water for drinking and cooking is essential. **Running the tap** when you prepare vegetables or other food is one of the most common ways to waste water. Half fill the sink with water for these jobs.

◇ Use the **leftover water** from jugs and kettles to water your indoor plants or your herb garden. Leftover water can also go on the garden if you don't use harsh detergents.

◇ **Dishwashers** are great water wasters. They are high in energy use and rely on particularly harsh detergents. If you need a dishwasher, buy a water/energy-efficient model and only use it when you have a full load.

◇ **Waste disposal units** are a two-way waste. They use energy and water (about 30 litres per day), and the food scraps they swallow up make valuable composting material.

BATHROOM

Turn the tap off when you brush your teeth and take shorter showers. About 30 litres of water per minute rushes down the drain – a few minutes here and there will make all the difference.

Bathing accounts for the largest share of household water use at over 25 per cent. There are many ways you can reduce your water consumption and still be clean.

◇ **An average bath** contains enough water to keep a shower running for 15 minutes – shower don't bathe. Save baths for those special occasions when you want to pamper yourself.

◇ Try to reduce the length of time you spend in **the shower** – cutting down by only 2 minutes will save 60 litres of water.

◇ Water-efficient **shower heads and aerators** use 2-5 times less water without any noticeable reduction in pressure.

◇ When **washing your hands**, half fill the basin then turn the tap off.

◇ Don't leave water running when **cleaning your teeth**. This wastes more water than a person in a Third World country uses in an entire day.

◇ Fix **dripping taps** immediately – they waste millions of litres annually. Even a very slow leak can waste over 1000 litres per month.

TOILET

Toilet flushing accounts for almost as much of our domestic use as bathing does – around 25 per cent.

Reduce this waste of water by buying a water-efficient unit.

When you install a new unit, choose a model with a half flush option. The new air-assisted models are designed to use up to 90 per cent less water.

NO ARTIFICIAL COLOURING-NO PRESERVATIVES NO ANTIOXIDANTS

LAUNDRY

The laundry is the next thirstiest room in the house.

◇ Use your **washing machine** only when you have a full load and reduce the amount of harmful chemicals you use.

◇ **When it's time to buy** a new washing machine buy an energy-efficient model that gives you a half load/short cycle option.

◇ **Top-loading machines** use more water than front-end loaders – up to 270 litres per load. A twin tub uses around 80 litres per load.

◇ **Reuse your washing water**. You can throw it on your garden (but only if you use very mild detergent or pure soap), wash the car with it or even the floors.

OUTDOOR

Although outdoor water use doesn't account for a large proportion of overall domestic use, it's an area where a high percentage of the water used is wasted.

◇ Avoid **washing the car** unless there's a real need. Use a bucket for washing and the hose only for rinsing. Hundreds of litres are wasted while the hose lays idle.

◇ Don't hose the driveway and paths. **A good, stiff broom** will clean them much more effectively.

◇ Install **rainwater tanks** – the extra water can be used for drinking or for rinsing hair for that special glow.

◇ For maximum absorption, **water your garden in the early morning** or late afternoon/early evening. If you water in the heat of the day most of the water will evaporate. Your garden only needs one good soaking a week. Frequent watering will encourage thirsty plants.

◇ Use **mulch** – it increases the benefit of the water you use by reducing evaporation.

◇ When you use a **sprinkler** remember to move it around and to turn it off. Automatic timers can take the guess work out of this.

◇ **Drip watering systems** are the most water-efficient option for watering your garden – they slowly release drips to the base of plants where the water is needed most.

OUR OCEANS

Seven-tenths of the planet is covered with oceans that make up one continuous ecosystem. Pollutants entering the system in one part of the world are detected in marine life thousands of kilometres away.

Oceans contain a multitude of diverse and rich environments, only a fraction of which have been explored. Some areas flourish with marine life while others are barren stretches of underwater sand. The Great Barrier Reef in Australia is the aquatic equivalent of a teeming rainforest and is home to over 3000 different species.

Every pollutant we add to our oceans has an adverse effect on the future resources the sea can offer. You can help by following these guidelines:

◇ Avoid using toxic chemicals – they make their way into the system via airborne pollution or runoff.

◇ Think before you flush!

◇ Support campaigns to save threatened wildlife habitat areas.

◇ Lobby your local council for a better sewerage system.

◇ Boycott companies known for pollution and dumping waste.

Primary Treatment (Screens) Remove only Solids

Secondary Treatment (biological) Removes organic matter and bacteria

Tertiary Treatment (biological & chemical) Removes most impurities

... GROW YOUR OWN ...
HEALTHY GARDEN

- ❖ **Growing your own food**
- ❖ **Organic gardening**
- ❖ **Companion planting**
- ❖ **Garden helpers**
- ❖ **Organic alternatives to chemicals**
- ❖ **Herb gardens**
- ❖ **All about compost**
- ❖ **Garden alphabet of herbs**
- ❖ **Watering your garden**
- ❖ **Using chemicals**
- ❖ **Garden design and equipment**
- ❖ **Choosing your lawn**

Your garden – whether it's in your backyard, or on a balcony or window sill – is a part of the environment that you have almost complete control over.

❖ FOOD FOR THOUGHT ❖

This section looks at your garden and the wonderful things that you can grow there. Hints include organic recipes for pest control, making your own compost and special tips on companion planting and herbs.

With a little thought and tender loving care, you can transform your patch into a lush, organic garden – one that is healthier, cheaper to run and more productive.

ORGANIC GARDENING
You can grow your own food and flowers successfully without using methods or substances which will damage the environment, or harm more than the pest you're aiming for!

Keep your garden healthy and free of poisons. Think of it as a microcosm of the broader picture. Organic gardening is all about using natural, organic methods to gain the best results.

Help your garden grow by recycling nutrients – compost your household scraps and garden waste. Include a variety of plants, trees and groundcovers, especially natives as this will encourage wildlife to visit your garden.

Arrange your garden to include the right combination of flowers, herbs, fruit and vegetables – this diversity will act as a natural form of pest control and promote a beneficial growing environment.

10 GOLDEN RULES

◆ **Plant a variety of native shrubs and trees**
◆ **Avoid chemical pesticides – use the safe, non-toxic alternatives**
◆ **Don't overwater your garden**
◆ **Install solar garden lights**
◆ **Reuse non-toxic washing water on the garden**
◆ **Don't burn rubbish in your backyard**
◆ **Make your own compost**
◆ **Plant deciduous trees for natural weather control**
◆ **Fit sprinkler systems with automatic timers**
◆ **Keep your lawn small enough to be managed with a hand mower**

TREES

Trees help to maintain the natural balance of gases in the atmosphere by extracting carbon dioxide (CO_2) from the air and using it for their own growth. The world's forests are our main natural defence against the buildup of CO_2 and they are being destroyed at an alarming rate.

Your garden has a vital role in cleaning the air you and your family breathe, so plant more trees and shrubs where you can and take care of the ones you have. A young tree will be a welcome gift for friends establishing a new garden.

Reduce your energy bills by planting deciduous trees in well-chosen spots around your house – they provide shade in summer, and reduce reflected heat from the ground while allowing winter sun into the house.

GOOD FAST FOOD

How often in your busy schedule have you taken the easy way out and bought your fruit and vegetables in a rush, without looking at either the price or the quality?

Although it seems like the only option at the time, convenience buying can become a very expensive habit – and is it really the easy way out? Especially when you arrive home only to find that your shopping looks as tired and colourless as you feel!

Most gardeners will tell you how therapeutic and rewarding their gardens are. The fact is, gardens also pay for themselves many times over. Once established, a garden can take as little as an hour a week to maintain. Think about how many hours a week you spend shopping when you could be watching your garden grow. There are many reasons why an organic garden makes sense.

Pesticide free

Many pesticides don't break down and remain poisonous for a long time. When your household garden is pesticide free, you can be sure that it is a safe place for children, family pets and wildlife, and that the food you grow is 100 per cent health-giving.

Money in the bank

A well-planned, attractive vegetable garden can be a great investment as well as a plentiful food source. Watch your food bills go down as the value of your property goes up.

One packet of seeds on average produces enough to feed

a whole family – a single packet of tomato seeds will normally produce around 100 plants.

Freshness you can taste

Fresh from your own garden means really fresh, crisp and full of flavour. Shop-bought produce is often more than one day old, and in some cases has been harvested several days earlier. If produce is on sale out of season, most likely it has been picked green, ripened artificially and transported over a vast distance.

Luxury of choice

Commercial growers tend to stick to popular varieties of fruit and vegetables that guarantee a high return. Some of the less common varieties are not so commercially viable.

When you have your own garden you can try more unusual or otherwise expensive varieties, selecting with your palate rather than your purse. This is particularly true of herbs, many of which are only available in dried form.

❖ GREEN AND CLEAN ❖

Although no-one wants their garden crawling with pests, it's important to remember that wildlife and insects are all part of your garden's natural food chain. Learn to identify and encourage the beneficial kinds which help to control pests.

Keep a diversity of plants – you can control common pests naturally by arranging your garden to include the right combination of herbs, flowers, fruit and vegetables. Because some plants act as natural pesticides, companion planting is one of the best ways to ensure healthy growth.

COMPANION PLANTING

Many plants have chemical defences against pests and diseases – they give off odours that either attract or repel certain insects. An abundance of different plants in your garden creates such a confusion of odours that insects are not so able to hone in on the plants

GOOD COMPANIONS PLANTING GUIDE	
VEGETABLE	**COMPANION**
asparagus	tomato, calendula
beans	stawberries, potatoes, leeks, eggplant, rosemary, rhubarb, marigold
beet	onions
broccoli	onions, aromatic herbs
brussels sprouts	aromatic herbs, onion, garlic
cabbage	aromatic herbs, onion, garlic, celery, peppermint, rosemary, sage, thyme
carrots	leeks, chives, lettuce, peas
cauliflower	aromatic herbs, onion, garlic
cucumber	corn, dill, radish, zinnias, sunflowers
garlic	roses
leeks	carrots
lettuce	cabbage, shallots, broccoli, radish
melons	zinnias
onions	cabbages
parsley	asparagus, celery, leeks, peas
parsnips	tomatoes
peas	carrots, potatoes
potato	horseradish, garlic
pumpkin	corn, radish
radishes	lettuce, mint
spinach	strawberries
squash	zinnias
tomato	basil, parsley, chives, asparagus
Note: Don't plant cabbage or fennel with tomatoes, radish or marigolds.	

they like. Some plants also grow better in association with certain other plants. Strawberries benefit from growing near borage, sunflowers grow well near cucumber and sweetcorn near pumpkin and marrow. Garlic and onions have special germicidal and fungicidal properties and can be planted throughout the garden (also excellent mixed in natural sprays with water).

Most of the aromatic herbs are natural insect repellents. Sage, rosemary, thyme and peppermint deter slugs and cabbage butterflies, lavender helps control ants and keeps the aphids away from your roses.

GARDEN HELPERS
Your garden has more friends than it does enemies – less than one per cent are actually pests. Find out how particular insects fit into your garden ecosystem before you target them as 'enemies'. They could turn out to be helpers.

◇ **Some insect-eating birds** consume over 100 insects a day. Entice them with a bird bath (which must be full of water even in winter), a bag of bird nuts or seeds suspended from a branch and an occasional snack of bread crumbs. If you find these visitors are more interested in your fruit trees, hang protective netting over the trees while they are bearing fruit.

◇ **Rocks, wooden boards, logs and barks** make good homes for other insect-eating guests like lizards, beetles and spiders.

◇ **Birds, frogs, toads and insects** like the pretty ladybird all help to control aphids and other pests. Encourage friendly insects to come into your garden.
Bacillus controls cabbage white butterfly, ermine diamond black and winter moths and black antworm.
Encarsia controls greenhouse whitefly.
Lacewing controls summer eggs of red spider mites, caterpillars, scales, whitefly thrips, mealy-bugs and leafhoppers.

FERTILISERS
A healthy garden, apart from being free of pests and pesticides, also needs to be fed. Opt for natural fertilisers that you can make yourself or, in some cases, buy commercially.
◇ Animal manure is the most traditional natural fertiliser – leave it to rot for a while before using it.
◇ Liquid plant manure is made by soaking green cuttings (like camphor) in a barrel of water.
◇ Seaweed and wood ash are both excellent sources of potash.

Ladybirds control scales, mealy-bugs, thrips, mites and aphids.
Mantids control eggs, scales, grasshoppers, moths, aphids, beetles, grubs, ants, leafhoppers, mealy-bugs and wasps.
Orchard bugs control aphids, scales, apple suckers, capsid bugs, caterpillars, pear midges, apple blossom weevils, mites and winter eggs of the red spider.

◇ **Attract beneficial insects** into your garden with a mixture made up of one part honey, one part brewers yeast and three parts water.

❖ ORGANIC ALTERNATIVES ❖

There are many natural ways to control garden pests and maintain a healthy garden without using chemicals.

One of the easiest ways to get rid of pests is to pick them off plants by hand (make sure you wear gloves). Aphids can be removed by rubbing with a small soft brush or with your fingers, caterpillars can just be picked off.

Lay planks or boards between rows of vegetables – snails will gather underneath them and can be picked off daily and disposed of in a bowl of salty water.

RECIPES

There is an enormous range of organic deterrents you can make yourself. But remember, don't spray unless you have to. Even safe, organic sprays are designed to kill the target, so do your homework and make sure you're killing the right insect.

Barrier bands: Barrier bands wrapped around the trunks of fruit trees will help prevent crawling insects from reaching the fruit and leaves. Make the band from an old cotton sheet or a piece of sacking. The insects hibernate in the band. Remove it regularly to dispose of the catch.

Beer traps (slug tubs): These are very effective against slugs. Mix up one part beer to two parts water and add a little brown sugar. Pour into a saucer nestled into the soil so the lip is level with the ground and remove the slugs daily. Alternatively, fill an old bottle with the same mixture and sink to ground level, emptying occasionally.

Chilli mix: This works well on ants and caterpillars. It is made from blending 2-3 fresh chillies with water and pure soap. This mixture also acts as a repellent in the kitchen. Also try blending 2-3 chilli peppers, half an onion and a clove of garlic in water, boil, steep for 2 days and strain. This spray won't damage plants and freezes well for later use.

Chives: Chives can be grown throughout the garden as an insect repellent and work particularly well planted at the base of fruit trees. Make up a garden spray by steeping a handful of chives in boiling water for an hour.

Citronella oil: Citronella oil is an effective personal insect repellent when rubbed on the skin. Unfortunately its strong odour is likely to repel more than just insects!

Garlic: Garlic is renowned for its insecticidal properties. Make up a good all-round spray by soaking 50 g of chopped garlic with a tablespoon of mineral oil and 250 mL of water. Allow the

MINI-GARDENS

Anyone can have a small garden – even if you don't have one square centimetre of backyard you may have a balcony or a sunny window sill. All you need to create a garden are plants, sunlight and water.

Fences, walls and balconies can be adorned with climbing plants – providing frames for foods like passionfruit, peas, tomatoes, beans and grapes.

Grow a selection of herbs and berries or tomatoes from hanging baskets – these look attractive and make a highly portable garden. Even fruit trees can be grown in pots on a balcony or rooftop, or in a small courtyard.

If you have a sunny window sill, grow your herbs in pots, and change them around regularly so that they all get their fair share of sunshine. Choose aromatic herbs like basil and several varieties of mint as these herbs are natural insect repellents (basil repels house flies, mint keeps ants and caterpillars at bay).

mixture to stand for 48 hours then filter. To make a spray, add 3 tablespoons of this concentrated solution to 1 litre of water. Garlic is also effective planted throughout the garden.

Grease: Ordinary axle grease smeared around the base of fruit trees will help prevent crawling pests like caterpillars and mites from reaching the fruit.

Herbs: Herbs act as natural insect repellents – plant them throughout your garden and use them in herbal sprays. (See pages 62-69.)

Hot water: Hot water has a fatal effect on many insects. Soft-bellied insects can't survive temperatures over 45°C, and beetles will die at 54°C. These temperatures won't harm even the most delicate plant.

Marigolds: Marigolds are excellent planted throughout the garden. The pungent secretions of certain marigold species mask the odours that attract many harmful insects.

Milk: Milk is a versatile garden spray. Make up a simple solution of one part milk to two parts water.

Onion: Onion is an effective repellent. Pour 500 mL of boiling water over 1kg of chopped onions and stand for 24 hours. Strain and dilute with 20 litres of water. This is particularly good for the control of sucking insects like aphids, thrips, mites and scale. To use, pour about 600 mL around each of the affected plants and repeat every 2 weeks until clear.

White pepper: White pepper dusted on vegetables will deter caterpillars.

Salt: Salt can be sprinkled directly onto pests, or used as a spray. Mix 50 g of salt with 4 litres of water. Particularly good for caterpillar control. Overuse can cause salinity problems.

Pure soap: Pure soap is an essential ingredient for many sprays. Mix with 9 litres of water to make up a spray – effective for control of aphids, caterpillars and whitefly.

Washing soda: Washing soda is effective against fungi and mildew. Mix 250 g of washing soda with 11 litres of water and 125 g of soft soap. Don't use this mixture in very hot weather.

Safe commercial preparations: These are also viable alternatives to homemade mixtures. One of the most popular organic insecticides is Derris dust, made from the Derris vine. Note that Derris dust comes in two forms: one synthetic, the other naturally-occurring. Commercial preparations can be very effective but must be used carefully, and only on affected plants.

If you are keen to learn more about natural forms of pest control and organic gardening, why not join an organic gardening club? It will give you the opportunity to link into a network of people with a vast collective knowledge.

WILDLIFE

Encourage and protect native flora and fauna whenever you can – their fragile ecosystems are continually under threat. Find out what trees, shrubs and other vegetation your local wildlife prefer to feed on and nest in. If you have the space, build a pond – this will attract several species of wildlife.

Train your pets not to attack birds or small animals. Attach a little bell to your cat's collar so that when it goes hunting the bell will warn prospective prey. Cats tend to hunt birds during the day and mice at night.

When you feed wildlife make sure the food isn't harmful to them in any way. Ask for more information at your local zoo or wildlife sanctuary.

❖ HERB GARDENS ❖

*Herbs act as natural deterrents to many insects.
Whether you plant them among your vegetables and flowers,
or keep them in pots on a window sill, herbs form a useful
and enjoyable part of any edible garden.*

GROWING HERBS INDOORS

Herbs generally love the sun. If you have a sunny window sill, grow some of your herbs in pots for variety, making sure they all get enough sunshine.

Keep a selection of your favourite culinary herbs in pots near your kitchen, as well as in the garden. Potted herbs kept indoors for any length of time may start to look a little droopy. Pop them outside for a day or two and they'll perk up almost immediately.

DRYING AND STORING HERBS

If your herb garden is flourishing and you have an abundance of herbs, why not dry and store them for later use?

Herbs should always be cut in dry weather – in the morning after the dew has dried off, but before the sun has robbed them of their essential oils. Once cut, tie the herbs in small loose bundles and hang them up in your garden shed or in an out-of-the-way corner in the laundry. They can also be spread on a wire-mesh rack and turned daily.

When herbs have dried, strip leaves from stems and store in airtight glass containers. Never store your dried herbs in paper bags – the paper will absorb the essential oils and flavour. Remember to label your herbs clearly as they are hard to identify in their dried state. Always store dried herbs in a dark cupboard.

MEDICINAL HERBS

There are a whole range of simple herbal remedies you can draw on if you have a herb garden.

Bad breath: Boil thyme and water for a few seconds. Let mixture steep for 10 minutes. Use half as a gargle and drink the other half. Peppermint tea is also good for bad breath. Make tea by adding a good teaspoon of peppermint (dried or fresh) to a cup of boiling water. Leave for a few minutes, strain and drink. Sweeten with lemon or honey to taste. Chewing fresh mint or parsley is also very effective.

Sore throats: Gargle with sage or thyme tea for relief from a sore throat.

Soothing baths: Aromatic baths are so soothing after a long, hard day. To make up a relaxing bath, add a large bunch of your selected herb to 1 litre of boiling water. Cover and allow to simmer for about 20 minutes, then strain and add to your hot bath. Rosemary is invigorating, thyme is good for aching muscles, lavender will relax you.

Aromatic rubs: To make an aromatic rub, add about 30 g of herbs to 200 mL of olive or vegetable oil. Heat mixture over a pan of boiling water for about 2 hours then strain. Thyme, rosemary and bay can all be used to make a soothing and fragrant rubbing oil. Make rubbing oils in large batches as they are fairly costly in time and energy to prepare. Aromatic rubs are ideal Christmas gifts.

Note: You can also grow comfrey, chamomile and valerian for medicinal purposes.

ALL ABOUT COMPOST

Composting is probably one of the simplest and most effective ways to enrich garden soil naturally. Healthy soil is the essential ingredient needed for healthy plants. Recycling your organic household wastes from the kitchen into the garden via a compost heap will save you an enormous amount of time, money and energy. The time and effort needed is really no more trouble than putting food scraps in the bin.

Start with a container that you keep handy in the kitchen or use a bowl that you add to a larger container kept outside the back door. Put all your organic kitchen scraps into this, including egg shells, tea leaves, vegetable peelings, coffee grounds, nut shells, fruit skins, small pieces of meat and small bones. Avoid putting large bones in as they take a long time to break down. If you don't have a dog there's bound to be one in your neighbourhood who would appreciate it!

You can add all manner of organic materials to your compost – natural fibre clothing, food-soiled paper, garden trimmings, wood shavings and grass from mowing the lawn.

MAKE YOUR OWN COMPOST

There are several methods to choose from when making a compost. The ideal method is to construct a wooden frame to contain the heap. Alternatively, you can dig a pit and make your compost in this or use the flat method by clearing the required surface area and building up your compost pile on it. Your local nursery or hardware store will also have a selection of commercial compost bins to choose from.

If you have a large garden, you may need more than one compost heap, thereby ensuring a steady supply of fertiliser for your garden and pot plants. Even if you're not the gardening type you can dispose of your organic waste by using the same method – it will just rot down. Simply dig a hole and throw your organic waste into it. When the hole fills up, cover it over and dig a new one.

◇ Form your compost in layers as this allows the air to circulate. The first layer should be made up of twigs and branches, the next layer of lawn and garden clippings then organic kitchen and household waste. Follow this with a layer of soil and some manure or a handful of lime to 'activate' the heap.

◇ Repeat the layers. If the material or matter used in the layers is dry, sprinkle with a little water.

◇ Spread the compost with a final layer of soil and cover with a lid of some sort – an old carpet, heavy sacking or a large sheet of plastic. This cover has several useful functions: it helps to maintain heat, prevents the wind from blowing the pile around, waterproofs the compost and discourages flies.

Allow 3-6 months for a 1.5 m compost heap to rot down.

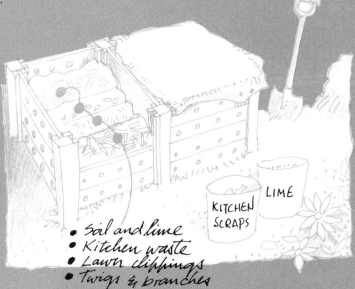

- Soil and lime
- Kitchen waste
- Lawn clippings
- Twigs & branches

LIME

KITCHEN SCRAPS

❖ GARDEN ALPHABET OF HERBS ❖

Growing herbs for cooking and other uses is as easy as A,B,C.
If you haven't got a garden, grow your herbs in an old tub
or in pots on a sunny window sill.

Herbs can transform ordinary foods, and always add that special 'je ne sais quoi' to your favourite dishes. The amount used in cooking depends on individual taste and on the type of herb. Strongly flavoured herbs such as bay, sage, thyme, oregano and rosemary should be used sparingly. Herbs have also been used for centuries to promote good health.

Fresh herbs should be chopped only at the last moment so that the full flavour of the aromatic oils is captured in the dish. Fresh herbs go well with vegetables and can often be used as a seasoning instead of salt. Basil and savory are a boon to people on low-salt diets. Many fresh herbs such as caraway, chervil, lemon balm, salad burnet, savory and sorrel are not readily available from the local fruit and vegetable market but can all be grown easily and quickly in your garden or on the kitchen window sill. Remember that the flavour of dried herbs is more concentrated so you should use them in smaller quantities.

MORE ABOUT HERBS

◇ Fresh herbs can be dried or frozen for winter use.

◇ Basil, thyme, majoram and nasturtium can be used as a pepper substitute.

◇ Herbs can be used to replace salt intake: try lovage, thyme and marjoram.

◇ Scatter edible flowers over salads: marigolds, nasturtium and the blue flowers of borage all look fantastic used this way.

◇ Comfrey makes an excellent liquid fertiliser with a high potash content. Steep leaves in hot water for 24 hours. Bottle in an airtight container and dilute in the ratio of 1:10 leaves to water.

ANGELICA
(Angelica archangelica)

This is a stout biennial or perennial herb which grows to 2 m or more. Leaves are pinnate and soft green, stems are round, ribbed and hollow. Flowers are yellow-green in umbels. Best suited to cool climate areas where it can be planted in sun or semi-shade. Shelter from strong wind is desirable because the stems are brittle.

USES: Angelica stems can be candied, and can also be used instead of sugar when stewing sour fruits like rhubarb. The roots are edible and can be served as a vegetable. Cook tips in jams and marmalade. The seeds are used in flavouring gin and some liqueurs. The roots can be dried then ground or powdered to use as a fixative in pot pourri. The dried leaves, flowers and seeds can all be used for pot pourri and herb pillows.

BASIL
(Ocimum basilicum)

An annual to 60 cm high with peppery, clove-scented leaves. Grow from seed in a sunny, moist but well-drained position sheltered from wind. Remove flower buds to encourage longer life.

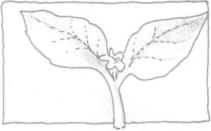

USES: Use only fresh basil leaves as it loses its flavour when dried. Excellent with all tomato dishes and torn up in salads. It goes well with carrots, zucchini, pasta sauces and chicken. Basil can also be used to keep flies and mosquitoes at bay.

BAY
(Laurus nobilis)

A slow-growing evergreen tree with aromatic leaves. Makes a good ornamental pot plant in a sunny sheltered position. Young plants need protection from frosts.

USES: Once established, the leaves can be harvested at any time of the year and used dried. A bay leaf is one of the three herbs that make up the classic bouquet garni. Use with tomatoes and beetroot and to flavour soups, sauces and stews. Add bay leaves to stores of flour, pulses and similar foods. They can also be used as an ingredient in pot pourri.

BORAGE
(Borago officinalis)

Borage is a coarse, thick annual, with a single tap-root, and branching hairy stems. Height varies from 30-90 cm. Leaves are greyish-green, about 10-15 cm long, Star-like summer flowers in white or blue are most attractive. Flowering can continue through winter in mild areas.

USES: Flowers and leaves can be eaten, although the hairs on the foliage become stiff and unappetising as the plant ages and only the young leaves should be picked. Finely chop the slightly cucumber-flavoured foliage and use as a garnish in salads. The flowers can be candied. Dip flowers and leaves in a light batter and deep fry.

CARAWAY
(Carum carvi)

A handsome biennial to 60 cm high with finely cut leaves and clusters of white flowers which produce aromatic seeds with their characteristic flavour. Sow seeds direct in spring or autumn. Needs a sunny, well-drained position protected from wind.

USES: Young leaves are used as a garnish for cooked vegetables. The seeds are used in dishes of cabbage, potatoes and parsnips. Also used in some cakes, biscuits and apple pie. Leaves and softer stems can be eaten in salads or cooked with other vegetables. Chew caraway seeds to dispel the odour of garlic and generally to sweeten the breath.

CHAMOMILE
(Anthemis nobilis)

A low-growing, creeping, branched perennial about 15-20 cm tall. There are two forms, single and double flowered. German chamomile *(Matricaria recutila)* is an aromatic annual herb which grows 15-60 cm high. The flowers are typical, white daisy flowers. Can be grown in sun or semi-shade. Not fussy about soil types but should never be allowed to dry right out. It needs well-drained soil.

USES: German chamomile is the one usually used medicinally and the tea, thought to be a curative and soothing drink, is made from the dried flowers.

CHERVIL
(Anthriscus cerefolium)

A small spreading annual to 50 cm. Fernlike leaves have a delicate aniseed flavour. Grow in a partially shaded position in a rich, moist soil.

USES: Chervil is used extensively in French cooking. Leaves are delicious with salad greens and spinach. Use in dressings, garnish for soups and with fish dishes.

CHIVES
(Allium schoenoprasum)

A perennial plant with hollow onion flavoured leaves and attractive mauve flowers. Sow seeds in a sunny spot to form a clump. Provide a moist, rich soil. In cold climates, chives die back in winter.

USES: Chives contain iron, pectin, sulphur and a mild, natural antibiotic. They help break down fatty foods, making them a useful herb to sufferers of high blood pressure. Chives are said to stimulate the appetite, hasten recuperation, ease the pain of rheumatism and gout, and cleanse the kidneys. Use to flavour potatoes, any of the marrow family and in fresh salads. Good in most savoury dishes and excellent with eggs and cream.

COMFREY
(Symphytum officinale)

Common comfrey is a large-leafed perennial with strong root development. It can be a nuisance if not kept under control. Average height is 60-90 cm. Plant comfrey in the shade. A rich, damp soil gives best results. Use ample compost for feeding and keep flower buds picked off to prevent seeding. Comfrey is hardy but don't let it dry out.

USES: Comfrey can be used in a wide variety of medicinal forms and for a wide range of purposes. Comfrey tea is good for diseases of the lungs and should be freshly made as the liquid ferments quickly. Comfrey leaves can be used raw or cooked and are excellent in the preparation of garden compost. Roots are used to make pickles and for the brewing of a comfrey wine. Note: Comfrey can be dangerous if misused. Always consult a qualified medical practitioner or professional alternative practitioner before using comfrey to treat any illness.

CORIANDER
(Coriandrum sativum)

An attractive annual to 60 cm. Lacy foliage has a distinctive taste. Aromatic seeds follow pink and white flowers. Sow seeds direct in spring in a sunny position and water generously. Harvest seeds in autumn and dry in a light, airy position then transfer to an airtight container.

USES: Coriander seeds are good for the digestion, helping carbohydrates to break down in the body. Coriander is used to flavour and render certain medicines more palatable. Used in almost every Thai dish. Leaves are tasty in salads and as a garnish for pea soup. The seeds complement mushrooms, cauliflower, beetroot and celery. They are also used in curries, sausage making and as a flavouring in cakes.

DILL
(Anethum graveolens)

A fast-growing, upright annual to 90 cm. Feathery leaves and clusters of yellow flowers, followed by sharp-tasting dill seeds. Sow seeds direct in a sunny, well-drained soil. The seeds can be harvested.

USES: Dill seeds and leaves can both be eaten. They contain potassium, sodium, sulphur and phosphorus. Dill is said to relieve indigestion. Dill water, available from chemists, has long been used as a sedative for young children. Chopped dill leaves go well with potatoes. Fresh dill in salads can help you to digest raw vegetables. Seeds are used in chutneys, dill pickles and herb vinegar.

FENNEL
(Foeniculum vulgare)

Fast-growing tall annual to 1.5 m. It has bright green, feathery leaves and clusters of yellow flowers followed by aniseed flavoured seeds. Grow in a well-drained, sunny position and provide plenty of water.

USES: Chewing fennel seeds can be useful to stave off hunger pangs if you are slimming, or to vaporise mucus when you have a cold. Fennel is also used to strengthen eyesight. The leaves are used in salads, relishes and as garnishes. Both leaves and seeds are traditionally used with fish. Seeds are used in soups, sauces and with lentils, rice and potatoes. Also used in breads and cakes.

GARLIC
(Allium sativum)

A bulbous perennial plant with strap-like leaves that is very easy to grow. Plant separated cloves in early spring in a rich and well-drained soil, preferably in full sun. When the foliage has died down at the end of summer, the bulbs can be carefully lifted. Drain in a well-ventilated position.

USES: One of the most ancient herbs, known for thousands of years as a flavouring, and as an antiseptic and medicine. As a blood purifier, it can maintain a healthy body and is recommended as a regular part of your diet as a preventative medicine. It can also combat cold infections, expel worms, lower blood pressure, act as a decongestant and cleanse the skin. Garlic is a very effective natural insect repellent and should be planted throughout your garden. The peeled and chopped cloves of garlic are used to flavour nearly all savoury foods. It is essential to aioli, the garlic-rich mayonnaise and many salad dressings.

GINGER
(Zingiber officinale)

A tall perennial plant to 1.5 m high with spikes of white and purple flowers and aromatic rhimzomes. Prefers a hot, humid climate in a rich, well-drained soil, preferably in partial shade.

USES: Warms the stomach and stimulates the secretory juices, aiding purification of the body's system. Often recommended as a therapeutic drink for colds. Fresh grated ginger is particularly good with steamed or stir-fried vegetables, especially Chinese cabbage. Use also with marrow, onions and sweet potato. It is an essential part of many curries, pickles and chutneys. Dried, powdered form is used in baking biscuits and cakes.

HORSERADISH
(Cochlearia armoracia)

A hardy perennial with long, elliptical dark green leaves. It grows to a height of about 60 cm with erect stems and has small, scented, four-petalled white flowers. Often grown for its thick, fleshy, aromatic roots – hot, pungent and full of flavour. An open sunny position is best, with a deeply dug, fertile soil.

USES: Purifies the blood and clears the sinuses, providing a good all-round tonic and relief from colds. Also cures dogs' worms. Horseradish sauce uses grated roots mixed with cream or some similar viscous liquid. It must be used raw as the cooked roots lose their flavour. Roots can be grated and dried and stored in airtight containers for later use. The leaves are also pungent and tasty and can be chopped and used as a salad ingredient. The leaves were once used externally as a dressing to salve burns and skin wounds.

LAVENDER
(Lavendula angustifolia – English*),*
(L. dentata – French*),*
(L.stoechas – Spanish*)*

There are many different varieties, species and forms of lavender, differing in the size of the plants or the flower spikes, the colour of the flowers and the strength of the perfume. Mostly shrubby perennials which grow from about 30-90 cm high. English lavender has whitish leaves when young and become green later. French lavender has marginally toothed leaves that are densely woolly and grey to silvery grey. Spanish lavender, also known as French or Italian lavender, is more bushy and leaves tend to be more green-grey with dark purple, cone-like flowers with a tuft of purple bracts at the tip. Lavender enjoys the sun and an open position with rich, but well-drained limy soil. Keep plants well trimmed to prevent them from becoming too woody and straggling.

USES: Lavender was once used as a strewing herb to sweeten the atmosphere. Today the flowers are made up into perfume sachets to keep drawers and cupboards sweet smelling. Lavender is used in the preparation of toilet waters and perfumes. Flowers can be candied and used to make a lavender vinegar. Also useful as a moth repellent.

LEMON BALM
(Melissa officinalis)

A perennial to 90 cm. Dark green, crinkled leaves that have a strong lemon scent. Grow in a rich, well-drained soil in full sun. Pinch back in early summer to encourge new growth.

USES: Use only fresh leaves sprinkled over vegetable or fruit salads. Leaves will give a light lemon flavour to cool drinks and make a good herbal tea. Lemon balm is sometimes planted in orchards to attract bees to pollinate the fruit blossom.

LEMON GRASS
(Cymbopogon citratus)
A grass-like perennial to 3 m high with strap-like leaves and a delicious lemon scent. It forms a large clump in a sunny, warm position with plenty of water, but good drainage.
USES: Contains vitamin A and an aromatic oil often used in skin cosmetics. The fleshy white lower part of the leaves is used in South-East Asian dishes. It adds a tangy taste to salads and is a must for curries. Chop fresh leaves into the teapot to make a healthy infusion for bright eyes and clear skin.

LEMON VERBENA
(Aloysia triphylla)
Not strictly a herb, but a tall, deciduous shrub which grows to 3 m high or even more. It has narrow leaves in whorls of three or four. Leaves are approximately 8 cm long with a strong lemon fragrance. Flowers vary from white to mauve in clusters 10-20 cm long. A warm, full-sun, sheltered position is best, with an average well-drained loam.
USES: The leaves retain their lemon fragrance for months, and are used in pot pourri and sachets and for flavouring or making a fragrant tea.

LOVAGE
(Levisticum officinale)
A tall perennial plant to 2 m high with a strong flavour of celery. Grow in a rich moist soil in full sun or part shade.
USES: The tender leaves add a celery-like flavour to potato salads, green salads and sauces and maintain their flavour when boiled for long periods. Delicious on tomato sandwiches. Use also to flavour soups and stews.

MARIGOLD
(Calendula officinalis)
A very hardy, annual herb which grows to about 60 cm high. The pale green, oblong-oval leaves are about 5-15 cm long and flowers vary from 4-10 cm across. Give pot marigolds full sun and an average garden soil. They are very easy to germinate and grow. Pot marigolds require very little special care, other than dead-heading to prolong blooming, and watering in hot, dry weather.

USES: Marigolds have insect repellent qualities. Use the crushed flower petals in soups, stews, cheese, scrambled eggs, mayonnaise and salads. The flower petals give both flavour and colour when added to rice dishes, cakes and puddings. The petals can be dried and used to make a tea, or blended with oils to make an ointment which is said to clear the skin from old wounds and scratches. Also used as a rinse to condition and lighten blonde hair.

MARJORAM
(Origanum majorana)
A fragrant perennial plant to 75 cm high with small oval leaves and clusters of white or mauve flowers. Grow in full sun in a well-drained soil and keep trimmed to encourage fresh, compact growth.
USES: Has remarkable antiseptic qualities – a regular intake cleans the blood and keeps you free of tummy bugs. Chew the leaves to soothe a headache. Fresh leaves are used in tomato dishes, with any of the cabbage family and green beans. Finely chop in salads and salad dressings. Also used to flavour soups, eggs and stuffings for meat dishes.

MINT
(Mentha spp)
There are many varieties of mint, but spearmint *(Mentha spicata)* and applemint *(Mentha suaveolens)* are the two most commonly used in cooking. They are fast-growing perennials which prefer a rich, moist soil and light shade.
USES: Peppermint oil contains menthol, useful in the treatment of sprains, bruises, toothache and blocked sinuses. Peppermint tea aids indigestion, flatulence, improves the appetite and is a general tonic. Spearmint also makes a refreshing tea and aids digestion. Chop and use with peas, new potatoes, zucchini and mixed green salad. Also good in fruit salads, cooling drinks, jellies, vinegar and lamb sauce.

NASTURTIUM
(Tropaeolum majus)
Decorative, hardy annual grown as a climber and sprawler in gardens for its bright, gold, orange, red trumpet flowers and the round, green , soft leaves. Likes full sun, but can tolerate part shade. Any average garden soil will suit. If grown for flowers and fruit, a not too rich, well-drained, sandy soil on the dry side is ideal, but for leaves for salads, use a well-composted soil.
USES: Nasturtiums are rich in vitamin C. The leaves have a hot, peppery taste when chopped and added to a salad. They are a good substitute for watercress. The green seeds are a good substitute for capers. The seeds and the leaves can be finely chopped and blended into butters and cheeses for an extra-piquant flavour.

OREGANO
(Origanum vulgare)
A small spreading perennial to around 50 cm. Small, pungent leaves and tiny white or mauve flowers. Grow in a well-drained soil in a sunny position.
USES: The fresh leaves are used to season salads and many tomato dishes, especially tomato sauces used with pasta. It is also used with eggplant, beans, zucchini and cheese.

ORRIS
(Iris x germanica var. florentina)

Orris is a typical iris with the sword-shaped, flag-like leaves and beautiful flowers up to 60 cm tall. These iris do best in full sun. Give them a well-drained soil and avoid wet positions as they are susceptible to rhizome rot.

USES: Orris is the powdered, violet-scented rhizome of var. *florentina* of the popular garden irises. It is used in perfumery. The iris rhizomes are dried and ground and used in perfumes and pot pourris as a fixative, and for their violet fragrance.

PARSLEY
(Petroselinum crispum)

A biennial plant to 60 cm high with flat or curly leaves. Parsley is grown from seed which should be sown direct in spring and summer. Grow in a sunny position and keep up the water in dry weather.

USES: All varieties of parsley are excellent for good health – they are particularly good sources of vitamin A, C and iron. They also contain vitamin B, sodium, calcium and magnesium. Parsley keeps the digestive system in good working order and especially the kidneys. Munch a little raw parsley to sweeten the breath or drink parsley tea to remove excess body fluid. Parsley is one of the best herbs of all with many uses in vegetable dishes, salads, soups, fish sauces, casseroles and omelettes.

PENNYROYAL
(M.pulegium)

Pennyroyal is one of hundreds of species of mint. All the mints are perennials, either upright or prostrate growing, and have four-sided stems with parallel, opposite leaves on short stalks, and spikes of small white, pink or purple flowers. Pennyroyal is easy to grow and does well in a warm and sunny aspect. Must not dry out if placed in full sun. A few roots can be potted up and grown indoors for kitchen use during winter.

USES: Mints are well-known for flavourings, condiments, teas and for use in salads and sandwiches. Sprigs of pennyroyal can be used in the kitchen to keep mice away.

ROSEMARY
(Ruta graveolens)

A Mediterranean evergreen shrub to around 1.6 m high. It has shining aromatic leaves and pale blue flowers. Grow in full sun in a well-drained position protected from wind.

USES: Rosemary water revitalises the scalp and tones the skin. Its oil makes a wonderful hair conditioner and can be rubbed into forehead and temples to relieve a tension headache. Dried leaves add fragrance to pot pourri, sachets and moth bags. Use finely chopped fresh leaves to flavour peas, spinach and baked pumpkin and potatoes. Also used to flavour roast lamb, chicken, stuffings and sauces.

RUE
(Rosmarinus officinalis)

A hardy, decorative evergreen sub-shrub with shiny blue-green leaves. Rue grows about 90-120 cm high. Leaves are deeply cut into blunt-ended, spatula-shaped segments and emit a strong odour. Flowers are yellow, appearing in loose corymbs in summer. Rue needs full sun or semi-shade and will tolerate the poorest soils. Does well in well-drained, gravelly or coarse sandy soils. Shorten in spring to keep the bush compact and shapely.

USES: Rue is seldom used as a culinary herb because most people find the taste too strong. Sometimes a few chopped leaves are used in salads. Commonly used as a medicinal herb. and as an insect repellent.

SAGE
(Salvia officinalis)

A small perennial shrub with soft, grey-green leaves and blue flowers during summer. Grow in a sunny, well-drained position. Trim regularly. An attractive border plant. Provide plenty of water during summer.

USES: As a medicinal herb, sage is used as a digestive, a blood tonic, an antiseptic, a tooth cleaner and a hair tonic. Use chopped fresh leaves sparingly in salads, potato dishes and with cheese. Use with pork and veal and in seasoning.

SALAD BURNET
(Sanguisorba minor)

A low spreading perennial with attractive lacy leaves set in pairs along the stems. Leaves have a slight cucumber taste. Crimson flowers in summer. Grow in a sunny or partially shaded position in a well-drained humus enriched soil. Provide plenty of water during the growing season.

USES: Young, fresh leaves are used mostly in mixed green salads. Use to flavour vinegar, butter and herb butter. Holds its leaves through winter, and forms a delicious basis for winter salads.

SAVORY, SUMMER
(Satureja hortensis)

An annual to 60 cm high with bronze-green leaves and white or pale pink flowers in summer. Grow in a sunny, well-drained position with plenty of organic matter added.

USES: Summer savory annoys blackfly (on broad beans) and is traditionally served with broad beans, cooked green beans and green bean salad. Good in stuffings, rice, soups, sauces and stews.

SAVORY, WINTER
(Satureja montana)
A semi-prostrate perennial with narrow green leaves and pale blue flowers. Grow in a sunny, well-drained position with plenty of organic matter added.
USES: Particularly good used in stuffings, rice, soups, sauces and stews.

SORREL
(Rumex acetosa)
A perennial to 90 cm tall with large bright green, arrow-shaped leaves that have a pronounced lemon taste and are rich in vitamin C. Prefers a well-drained, rich soil in sun or semi-shade.
USES: The slightly bitter flavour in sorrel is oxalic acid, which gives this herb its wonderful blood-cleansing properties. Add a few leaves in the blender when making your healthy vegetable juice to keep your liver and kidneys in good working order. Use sparingly however as too much oxalic acid can cause poisoning and kidney problems. The leaves are also effective as a poultice for boils or other skin eruptions. Young fresh leaves are excellent in a mixed green salad. A few leaves can be added when cooking spinach. Used in the classic French sorrel soup. Use also in sauces and vegetable purees.

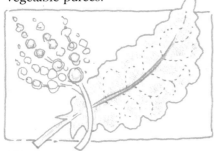

TANSY
(Tanacetum vulgare)
Common tansy is a coarse perennial herb with a grooved angular stem. Grows to about 90 cm or more. Attractive dark green, fern-like leaves. A shorter, more compact variety (*T.vulgare* var. *crispum*) is better as a garden plant. The flowers are like small, yellow buttons. Has a pungent, bitter odour. Grows in almost any soil and position – sun or part shade. Plant in an isolated bed or large planter box as tansy grows quickly and can over-run your garden.
USES: Tansy can be used in cooking, but only in very small doses. Large doses can be poisonous. Has medicinal properties, but should not be used without professional advice. Used as an ingredient in a tea or tisane. Flowers can be dried and used as perpetuelles. They and the leaves can also be used in pot pourri.

TARRAGON
(Artemesia dracunculus)
French tarragon is a bushy perennial to around 1 m high. It has dark slender leaves with a slight anise flavour. Grow in a moderately rich, well-drained soil in a sunny spot. French tarragon can only be propagated by division.

USES: Use with fish, shellfish, chicken, turkey, game, veal, liver, kidneys and in egg dishes. Tarragon vinegar is an essential ingredient in Bearnaise sauce.

THYME
(Thymus vulgaris)
A strongly aromatic shrubby perennial to around 45 cm high. It has tiny, oval leaves and bears pretty pastel coloured flowers. There are many varieties including lemon thyme, caraway thyme and a variegated type. All thymes like a sunny position with a light, well-drained soil. Trim to keep compact. Thyme is one of the most successful herbs for drying.
USES: Thyme has medicinal qualities as well as culinary uses, containing high concentrations of thymol, a powerful antiseptic. Thyme oil, applied to the forehead and temples, can soothe an aching head while thyme tea makes a refreshing antiseptic drink, clearing infections in the throat during a cold. Also aids digestion and bowel disorders. Use fresh leaves sparingly with most vegetables including beetroot, tomatoes and zucchini. Use in casseroles, meat dishes, pates and stuffings.

VALERIAN
(Valeriana officinalis)
A medium to tall perennial which can reach 1.5 m in height, with bright, green, divided and almost fern-like leaves and clusters of pale pink flowers. Grows wild in ordinary soil in moist, shady places, usually where the ground is stony or well drained. Plants are not fussy about soil, but allow plenty of space as they are comparatively large.
USES: The name comes from the Latin, *valere,* to be healthy. A nervine is produced from the plant which is said to induce sleep. Valerian has long been known as a sedative and painkiller. Infusions made from its roots should be taken with caution. Excellent in pot pourri and sachet mixtures. Cats are attracted by the scent of the root.

WORMWOOD
(Artemisia absinthium)
Wormwood is a coarse perennial herb which grows to about 50 cm in height. The stems are erect with dissected silvery-grey leaves, but the lower stems may be brown. The clusters of small green-yellow flowers grow in the leaf junctions. Does best in full sun and needs a well-drained soil.
USES: Wormwood foliage, dried and collected in sachets, can be used to ward off moths and household insects. Note: Wormwood can be dangerous if misused. Always consult a qualified medical practitioner or professional alternative practitioner before using wormwood to treat any illness.

❖ WATERING YOUR GARDEN ❖

It is easy to forget just how precious water is – when it's on tap the supply seems limitless. Try to use the minimum amount of water needed to do the job, and don't pollute the water around you in any way.

SIMPLE RULES

◇ **Don't over-water** your garden. Once established, one good watering a week is better than frequent sprinkling.

◇ **Don't water in the heat of the day** as the water will just evaporate. The best time to water for maximum absorption is late afternoon or early evening. If this doesn't fit in with your daily routine, water in the early morning.

◇ **Don't waste water.** Water that runs down paths and steps is wasted.

◇ **Look after established trees.** They provide shade for your garden beds and stop them drying out too quickly in summer.

◇ **Train your garden to use less water.** Reduce the amount you use gradually – your plants will let you know when you've gone too far.

◇ **Use mulch.** Mulching enriches the soil, reduces water evaporation and weed growth and insulates plant roots from rapid temperature changes.

◇ **Keep your soil well drained.** Damp and poorly drained soil attracts slugs, snails, millipedes and wireworms. Good drainage and aerating the soils with organic matter will prevent root rot and unwelcome visitors.

◇ **Try to incorporate hedges and windbreaks** into your garden design – wind can quickly dry out the soil.

◇ **Catch rainwater** for use in the garden by channelling water from gutters into a barrel or tank. Always cover any large water receptacles to prevent children or animals from falling in.

◇ Always observe **water bans**.

WATERING METHODS

Manual sprinklers: There is a huge variety of manual sprinklers available to choose from. Large sprinklers require strong water pressure to work efficiently so choose a smaller, simpler model. Move the sprinkler regularly to give a good distribution of moisture and don't forget to turn it off. Invest in an automatic timer or set an alarm in the house to remind you.

Automatic sprinklers: There is a tendency when using an automatic sprinkler system to over-water the garden. Over-watering not only wastes water but encourages a thirsty garden, drains the soil of nutrients and destroys soil texture. If you use an automatic system try to reduce the frequency and duration of watering and don't forget to turn the timer off in wet weather.

Soaker hoses: Soaker hoses are pricked with tiny holes that release a fine water spray. Don't forget to move them or switch them off.

Hand-held hose: Watering by hand is a time-consuming method but allows you to look at your plants and find any problems early. A hose uses much less water than a sprinkler system. Make sure you water in each area long enough to soak the ground. If you consistently under-water, your plants will develop shallow roots.

Drip watering systems: These are among the most water-efficient systems available. The tubing is dotted with small holes that release very slow drips of water to the base of plants. The water is directed exactly where it is needed and nothing is wasted.

Watering can: A watering can is good for lots of little jobs. It is excellent for watering house plants, small herb gardens, hanging plants and potted plants on your balcony or in the conservatory.

MULCH TIP

The most effective mulches are organic – autumn leaves, grass clippings, straw, softwood, sawdust, forest bark, newspaper – because they decompose into humus that in turn supports aerobic soil life and earthworms.

FACT

The manufacture of pesticides for use in agriculture is big business. In a single year over 40 million tonnes of insecticides, herbicides and fungicides are sold in world markets. Fifteen per cent of that is destined for domestic use.

The first use of DDT as an insecticide was in 1939 during World War 2 to control the epidemic of insect-carried diseases affecting troops. At the time it was considered miraculous because it killed the disease-carrying insects without harming the soldiers. It wasn't until 1954 that serious side effects were found.

DDT is only one of a group of pesticides, called chlorinated hydrocarbons, which don't break down and remain poisonous for as long as 30 years. DDT was banned in most countries in the 1970s. However, new pesticides are being developed all the time. Many of these chemicals are health hazards and cause a whole range of environmental problems – they leave dangerous residues in the soil, harm wildlife and cause atmospheric pollution.

IF POISONING OCCURS

✚ Call a doctor or ambulance. Administer First Aid immediately. Be guided by the instructions on the pesticide label.

✚ Induce vomiting if a pesticide has been swallowed but not if the victim is unconscious or if kerosene has been swallowed.

✚ If skin absorption has occurred, wash the affected areas thoroughly, including eyes if they have also been affected.

✚ If the victim is unconscious, apply mouth-to-mouth resuscitation and cardiac compression.

The doctor will need to have all the relevant information about the accident to choose the appropriate treatment, so note the trade name and common name of the chemical, amount taken, solvent used and a clear report of the symptoms as they occurred. Keep labels, containers and a sample of the vomit, if any, ready for analysis.

PESTICIDES TO AVOID

When you buy commercial pesticides always read the packet, and if the product contains any of the following chemicals, don't buy it. In fact, some of these chemicals have already been taken off the market.

Aldin	DDD	Lindane	Sulphate
Amitrol	DDT	Mercurial compounds	Tedion
Arsenical compounds	Dieldrin	Methoxchlor	Thallium
Azodrin	Endrin	Ovex	Thiodan
Bidrin	Heptachlor	Strobane	Toxophane
Chlordane	Kelthane		

❖ GARDEN DESIGN ❖

*If you have created a beautiful garden you'll want
to spend time outside enjoying it. Try to arrange your garden
so you have a sheltered alcove where you can enjoy the winter
sun, protected from prevailing winter winds – or a shady grotto
where you can sit out of the summer sun.*

If you buy timber garden furniture, avoid tropical rainforest timbers, both imported and local. Choose plantation timbers. If you buy plastic furniture look after it properly to ensure it lasts as long as possible (remember, it's made to last forever!).

CHEQUERBOARD HERB GARDEN

You can create a chequerboard by missing out square pavers or bricks in a path and planting the square of soil with herbs. Variations on this pattern, with just the odd paver missing, provide a less formal arrangement. Use only low-growing herbs, mint is ideal, as the pavers restrict its rampant root growth.

SOLAR LIGHTS

Solar garden lights store energy from the sun during the day and use this energy to light your garden at night. They are inexpensive and easy to install and have the added benefit of being mobile so you can move them around.

CONCRETE

Concrete or asphalt may cover around one third of the land in an average city but is out of place in your garden where natural textures, colours and forms predominate. Solid paving tends to block off natural drainage and kill the soil below. If you have an area you want to pave, look at some of the attractive, low-maintenance alternatives.

◇ **Old bricks or paving stones** can be set into the soil, creating a surface that still allows mosses and plants to grow in the cracks. The fragile balance of plant and insect life will be preserved while creating a firm, flat surface for pathways and al fresco entertaining.

◇ If you have vast expanses of concrete surrounding your home, **don't waste water** hosing it down – a good stiff broom is much more effective for cleaning.

GREEN AIR CONDITIONING

When we think of air conditioning most of us imagine machinery pumping out hot or cold air. There are other far more pleasant and effective ways of heating and cooling your garden and indoor living area. Why not incorporate some of these ideas into your garden design?

Shade houses: A simple pergola or conservatory built on the hottest side of your house can be adorned with vines and hanging baskets. This will filter the light reaching your home and keep it cooler in summer.

Greenery: Greenery around your home. Avoid the glare of paths and paving by shading them properly. Hedges will help shut out the harsh, reflected glare from bitumen roads.

Pots of water: Place pots of water below your windows in the path of summer breezes as a cooling aide.

Greenhouses: A greenhouse or conservatory attached to your home can take the chill off the entire house. Shut the door to the greenhouse in the early evening to trap the warm air.

Window greenhouses: A window greenhouse can be built in any window opening. A greenhouse which extends out about 60 centimetres from your window will provide you with extra warmth – and tomatoes all year round (all you have to do is plant them!).

Windbreaks: Position windbreaks to eliminate the prevailing winter winds and to reduce the effect of drying winds on your garden.

Sun traps: Sun traps absorb and re-radiate heat. Large dark pots or sand-filled tubes placed around your home will increase winter insulation.

Deciduous trees: Deciduous trees provide shade in summer and let the sun through in winter. Plant them strategically around your home.

Window pergola: Window pergolas are window boxes extended by latticework. If you cultivate climbing plants in the window box they will climb up the lattice, forming a living blind that will block direct sunlight. If you want to block the sun all year round, plant evergreens like passionfruit and ivy. If you only want to block the summer sun, plant deciduous vines – grapes, creepers and climbing beans.

There are many different styles of lawns, some which require a lot of work and others, like native landscape and wildflower lawns, which need less attention in the long run. Whether your lawn is the conventional turf-grass style or something less formal, it's not necessary to use enormous quantities of chemical fertiliser, herbicides and insecticides to keep it green.

If your lawn is in the wrong place, on poorly drained land or under trees, you will probably have problems no matter how many chemicals you use! Chemicals are generally not the solution.

◇ Choose your lawn plants carefully. You may need to select grasses which are tolerant of shade, poor soils and a dry or wet habitat. Another option is to try natural lawn substitutes – groundcovers like cotula, chamomile and periwinkle.

◇ You may opt for a native landscape or wildflower lawn in a small area where mowing is difficult or unnecessary. Consult your local nursery or plant shop about a suitable selection of seeds for native groundcovers and wildflowers.

◇ If you do have a turf-grass lawn, rake it once a month during the growing season. Aerate the soil well with a fork – compacted soil will result in waterlogging, browning and bare patches.

◇ When you mow your lawn, you actually remove nutrients. Recycle grass clippings in summer (not in winter, it may be too damp), and use organic manures.

◇ Although worms produce surface casts in lawns, they should not be considered pests. The casts make excellent fertiliser and worms help aerate the soil. Simply rake the surface casts away.

GARDEN EQUIPMENT

Buy good quality garden tools or equipment as they will need to withstand vigorous wear and tear. Ensure their long life by looking after them. Store out of the weather in your garden shed to help prevent metals rusting and wood cracking. Oil tools regularly, even timber handles. Don't stand your spade on the concrete floor as this will blunt the blade. Hang it on the wall or stand it upside down.

POWER TOOLS

All electric and petrol-powered machines make a considerable noise. In recent years, machines using sound absorption material and more efficient silencers have been developed.

If you are buying a new lawn mower or power tool, ask about its noise level. If you intend to hire a machine, ring around till you find a hire company that stocks properly silenced machinery.

Think of your neighbours and only use power tools at times that won't disturb them. Always avoid using tools in the early morning or at night. Most countries have noise control regulations. Find out what they are in your area and abide by them.

LAWN MOWERS

Lawn mowing is one of the best ways to ruin a peaceful Sunday afternoon – both for the person mowing the lawn and those who have to listen to the racket!

Ideally, keep your lawn small enough to be easily managed with a hand mower. Lawns are not only water guzzlers – mowing your lawn removes nutrients and contributes to the Greenhouse Effect.

Landscape gardens which incorporate native groundcovers and wildflowers need far less time and effort to maintain than conventional turf-grass lawns and will also attract wildlife into your garden.

BACKYARD BURNING

Don't burn rubbish in your backyard – it pollutes your neighbourhood and is a potential health hazard. Smoke from an ordinary garden fire contains around 70 ppm (parts per million) of cancer-causing benzopyrenes. Don't turn valuable humus into ashes, turn your garden wastes into compost.

LEISURE

- ❖ Tourism
- ❖ When on holiday
- ❖ Four-wheel drives
- ❖ Hunting
- ❖ Camping
- ❖ Fishing
- ❖ Boating

You have an impact on the environment whatever you do in your free time.

❖ ENJOY, DON'T DESTROY ❖

If you are lucky enough to have an annual holiday, reasonably free weekends and a forty hour working week or less, you probably have time to enjoy a wide range of leisure activities.

You have an impact on the environment whatever you do in your free time, whether it's walking, cycling, horseriding, camping, boating, waterskiing, holidaying in wildly exotic places, or simply staying at home to work in your garden.

This section includes a few tips on how to enjoy your leisuretime without endangering wildlife or harming the environment.

TOURISM

Tourism is the world's third largest industry and the economies of many countries depend on it. The tourist industry can work both for and against the environment.

In many cases, the growth of tourism has been one of the strongest arguments for the conservation of wilderness areas. At the same time, tourism has led to environmental problems that affect wildlife and their habitats, as well as the lives of indigenous people.

The souvenir trade in exotic goods is growing, despite moves to protect endangered species that fall victim to it. Even with world media coverage on the plight of the elephant and the

TRAVEL FOOD

No matter how you travel, food on the move is usually heavily processed, overwrapped and tasteless. Airports, train stations, bus terminals and fastfood truck stops all seem to offer a similar range.

Carry a small supply of food with you – even if it's only a bag of dried fruit or nuts – and a flask of water.

Travel with your own washable mug to avoid the disposable plastic kind – this saves waste and your drinks will taste better.

much publicised evils of the ivory trade, people still return from African holidays loaded down with ivory bracelets and trinkets.

The search for new tourist locations extends to the remotest corners of the globe, often resulting in species being driven from their remaining breeding sites. The Antarctic is one of the last and most rich wilderness areas left on Earth and it faces an uncertain future, despite strong moves to protect it.

WHEN ON HOLIDAY

When you visit friends, you treat them and their home with respect and courtesy. When you're on holiday a similar code should apply. If you leave anything behind it should be the memory of a smile or a kind gesture, not your name carved into a tree trunk or a pile of beer cans on top of a mountain.

◇ When you decide on your next destination, **spend time researching** the region beforehand. Find out about the people, their lifestyle and local customs. When you visit the area make an effort to minimise your impact.

◇ If you travel to a **Third World country**, choose accommodation that is locally owned and managed. It has been estimated that over 80 per cent of money paid to foreign-owned hotels leaves the country.

◇ **Choose a local tour operator** who is likely to put something back into the country's economy. Many African safari operators contribute money to conservation projects.

◇ If you go on a **novelty tour or adventure holiday**, like an African Safari, familiarise yourself with international wildlife laws, especially those dealing with trade in animal products. Any large conservation organisation will be able to help you with this.

◇ Be aware of any **environmentally sensitive areas** or endangered species in the regions you travel to. In the South Sea island of Vanuatu, for example, the coconut crab, a renowned culinary delicacy, has been exploited to such an extent that it is now facing possible extinction. Uninformed tourists, blissfully unaware of the crab's plight, feast on it daily.

◇ Never buy **souvenirs** that are made from any part of a wild animal. The case of elephants and ivory is a classic example of what can happen to a wildlife species in the race for tourist dollars.

◇ Never pick **wildflowers or plants** from native habitats.

◇ Don't take **plants or seeds** across borders without declaring them – the regulations controlling their import and export were established for good reasons.

❖ USING NATURAL AREAS ❖

One of the most important actions you can take to ensure that remaining natural areas are preserved is to use them. Every time you visit you are casting your vote for the future.

When you visit natural environments, take care not to disrupt these valuable ecosystems. Teaching children bush craft and how to respect nature is a move in the right direction.

◇ Stick to **established paths**.

◇ **Park the car and walk** rather than drive – it can be a very rewarding experience and is far less disruptive.

◇ Never pick **wildflowers** or take rocks.

◇ Don't take **your pets** with you. Your dog may be well trained but his scent alone will be enough to scare timid creatures.

◇ Always take your **litter** home with you. Litter can be a problem even in such remote places as the summit of Mt Everest.

FOUR-WHEEL DRIVES

Four-wheel drives can cause a whole range of environmental problems including soil erosion, damage to plants and wildlife. Always drive on the roads and tracks provided – never through virgin bush, wetlands or over beaches, cultivated fields or dunes.

HUNTING

Hunting should never really be referred to as 'sport'. Clay pigeon or target shooting is sport, but the hunting of animals for trophies has had a devastating impact on many species.

Inexperienced shooters can destroy animals caught in the crossfire, including quite rare species. Make sure you know what you're doing. Only shoot in season and know your species.

Study the birds' markings until you know them well enough to distinguish them in flight.

Lead pellets from shotgun cartridges create other problems for wildlife. Birds eat the pellets by mistake and can die from lead poisoning. If lead enters the waterways in large enough quantities it can affect an entire aquatic ecosystem.

Why not shoot with a camera instead of a rifle?

CAMPING

A camping holiday that takes you far from exhaust fumes, noise and telephones can be much more relaxing than a whirlwind package tour to a plush resort. Remember, don't take your pet camping and carry your litter home with you. Here are some camping guidelines:

◇ Avoid lighting **fires** close to tents.

◇ **Never leave a fire unattended** and make sure the fire is completely out before leaving.

◇ Don't waste **firewood**. Dead timber from the forest floor provides food and shelter for many native species and is part of the forest's humus layer.

◇ Don't wash yourself or utensils in **streams** that supply drinking water for other campers.

◇ Avoid using **harsh soaps and shampoos**.

◇ **Swim downstream** from where your drinking water is collected.

◇ Bury **excreta** not only away from camp sites but also well away from streams.

◇ **Food scraps** can be buried. Tins, plastic and paper should be carried out with you.

FISHING

The first rule of fishing should be to eat or give away what you catch!

◇ Dispose of your tangled and discarded scraps of **nylon fishing line**. If these offcuts are left lying around they can become tangled around the feet and wings of waterbirds.

◇ Practise a policy of **catch and release**. The more anglers do this, the more they contribute to the future of fishing. A released fish will most likely live to reproduce.

◇ An increasing number of saltwater anglers are tagging fish before releasing them, using special tags supplied by fishing authorities. This contributes immensely to the **collection of scientific data**.

◇ Only take enough fish for your immediate table needs and always **observe the legal sizes and restrictions** for different fish species. These guidelines were established to ensure fish populations remain at a sustainable level.

BOATING – SIMPLE RULES

◇ Bow waves made by speeding boats can cause damage to natural shorelines. **Slow down** on the water.

◇ **Never discharge your fuel** or engine oil into the water. Collect it in containers and dispose of it properly.

◇ When you spend the day on the water, never throw your litter overboard. **Take a box or a rubbish bag** on board with you and dispose of it properly when you get back home.

◇ Only use **non-toxic anti-fouling paints** to stop encrustations on the underside of your boat.

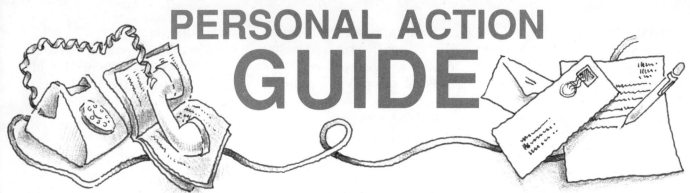

PERSONAL ACTION GUIDE

This book has dealt with all the practical things you can do to help keep the environment clean, from recycling food scraps through to buying an energy-efficient washing machine. As important as these things are, they are not the whole answer. It is important to become involved in environmental issues on a larger scale as well, within the community and beyond.

The first step is to learn about issues that are threatening the community, not only locally based but also from a global perspective. Stay informed by reading the newspapers regularly. Make sure you read the whole story so you have all the facts. If the issue you are concerned about is a general problem, spend some time at the library reading up on it. Many conservation groups have information they will send on request. If you are concerned about a community issue, local newspapers, councils or libraries will be a good source of information. Local action groups can also help.

◇ **Strategy:** When an issue arises that you feel you want to become involved in, plan your campaign carefully.

◇ **Research:** Some of the best sources for information include newspapers, libraries, controlling authorities and established action groups.

◇ **Define your objectives:** What are you trying to achieve?

◇ **Gathering support:** Enlist the support of other people or become involved with an existing group working to achieve the same goals. More people means greater collective knowledge to draw from. Each person will have something to contribute.

◇ **Develop your strategy:** Once you have determined your objectives, it will be far easier to achieve your goals.

TACTICS
◇ Write letters to the press.
◇ Interest the public, call a meeting.
◇ Contact other groups in an attempt to join forces on the issue.
◇ Write to the controlling authorities to voice your concerns and get their support.
◇ Organise direct meetings with government officials and/or developers.
◇ Seek radio or television coverage.
◇ Display posters/notices in public places.
◇ Distribute information pamphlets.
◇ Advertise and organise a survey. This will give you valuable information and the opportunity to gather more support.
◇ Take legal action (can be costly).
◇ Take direct action like a protest march or rally (use only as a last resort).

SUPPORT
When you decide to initiate a protest it is important to gather all the community support you can. Approach every level of the community including:
◇ individuals
◇ business and industry
◇ government agencies
◇ community groups (youth groups, community service groups, churches, sports clubs)
◇ schools and colleges including both teachers and students
◇ media (newspapers, TV, radio)

The type of support you may need includes:

◇ **Funding:** No matter how low-key your campaign is you will still need money for things like postage and stationery.

THE ART OF LETTER WRITING

Writing letters to marketing managers or the daily press is a very effective way of publicising your views. One of the most widely read sections of any newspaper is the *Letters to the Editor*.

Writing letters to politicians and officials is also very worthwhile. All mail sent through official channels is monitored to enable governments to respond to public opinion. When you write:
◇ be brief and concise
◇ include itemised points
◇ always have a subject heading
◇ have the letter typed
◇ sign your name, title and the name of your group
◇ write on recycled paper
◇ substantiate claims you make with reputable scientific references
◇ identify yourself as a ratepayer, customer or voter
◇ if you are responding to a government document, press report or any other written material, give all the details of the given document like title, date and page number
◇ when you write to a government department, always send a copy of your letter to the appropriate person in the opposition party
◇ keep a copy of your correspondence (the written word is far more powerful and binding and can be kept as a permanent record of your dialogue)
◇ follow up with a phone call

Here are a few examples of the thousands of problems you may want to write about:

To companies:
◇ wasteful extravagant packaging
◇ dangerous chemical additives
◇ polluting manufacturing plants
◇ noise pollution
◇ destroying natural habitats

To councils:
◇ conservation of natural areas
◇ improved bicycle and walking paths
◇ better recycling services
◇ improved litter control
◇ more bins on beaches and in parks
◇ spraying of poisons

To governments:
◇ better public transport systems
◇ protection of wilderness areas
◇ tougher pollution controls
◇ laws protecting endangered species

◇ **Equipment and supplies:** In many cases, the publicity that local businesses receive will more than compensate them for their donations.

◇ **Professional advice:** Often professional people like lawyers or business managers will offer free advice or services.

◇ **Labour:** The more people in your network, the more effective your campaign.

SPEAKING AND LOBBYING

Improved public education about environmental issues is vital. Your public spokesperson must have a thorough knowledge of the issue, be presentable in appearance and have a strong, interesting speaking style.

◇ Keep talks brief and to the point.

◇ Visual materials will increase the impact of your message.

◇ Distribute printed materials outlining the problem and your intended goals at meetings (include name, phone number and postal address).

◇ Ask for donations.

NEGOTIATION

Although it is sometimes difficult to stay calm when dealing with hostile or apathetic people, there is nothing to be gained by alienating them. Keep your adversaries fully informed of your policies and send them educational materials about the issues.

LEGAL ACTION

If you have someone from the legal profession involved in your cause, it may be viable to fight your case through the courts. Free legal advice along the

ETHICAL INVESTMENT

Have you ever thought about how your money is used when you tuck it away in the bank or building society? When your money goes into the bank you assume it will be invested wisely. The fact is, however, banks will lend money to anyone for any venture as long as they feel their money is secure.

The good news is that you now have an alternative – ethical or conscious investment – which enables you to invest in ventures which don't harm or exploit the environment, and which embody a responsible ethic. Major conservation groups will be able to give you more information about this.

A CASE STUDY

Let's look at a hypothetical situation that may threaten your local area and how you could campaign to save it.

The issue: It is proposed that a large local pond be filled in to allow for urban expansion. The pond is renowned in the area for the diversity of its bird life and is one of the only natural reserves of any significance left in your community. You are completely opposed to its development.

The campaign: Determine whether the proposed activity is covered by any existing council regulation or environment law. Find out who owns the habitat, and what its current zoning status is.

◇ *Find out who else is opposed* to this development. Contact local conservation groups, schools, birdwatching clubs or any other community-based organisation that you think may support your cause.

◇ *Gather information* on how this development will adversely affect both the community and wildlife.

◇ *Write letters* to the local newspapers outlining the issue and lobby the editor to run a feature story. Organise a rally at the pond to ensure you get press coverage.

◇ *Write to the relevant department* that is planning the development. Outline your arguments for preservation and ask them to reconsider their decision. If possible, suggest an alternative site.

◇ *Prepare a public display* to educate the public about the issue. Ask your local library if you can exhibit it there.

◇ *Organise petitions* and leave them in local shops for people to sign.

◇ *Involve a major environment group.* Even if they don't take up your banner, their advice will prove invaluable.

◇ *Present a united front* once you have rallied support and established who your allies are.

Your actions need not be at this level. There are plenty of other ways you can be involved. Why not instigate a cleanup day at your local lagoon or initiate a tree-planting weekend in a degraded reserve? Often local councils are happy to donate trees for this type of project.

Recycling your waste, saving energy and fuel, growing an organic garden, and limiting the amount of chemicals you use are all positive actions – every little bit helps.

---

way will be an added bonus. Often someone within your group will have a friend or relative they can call on for a quick legal appraisal. Not every cause will benefit by legal action, so don't waste your time, effort or money unless you have a good chance of winning.

DIRECT ACTION

Although direct action should always be your last resort it can be a very important and effective part of a campaign.

◇ When all other avenues of protest have failed, organised marches or protests can make all the difference and attract media attention or community support.

◇ Carefully plan protest action. Inform the press of the time and place of your protest, display banners and placards prominently and have an articulate speaker.

◇ Avoid causing any violence or offensive behaviour as this may jeopardise the success of your whole campaign. Witty grandstanding, on the other hand, may entice the media support needed.

BECOME INVOLVED IN LOCAL POLITICS

The most effective way to make changes to any system is to work from the inside. If you don't have time to get involved personally, support a local candidate who mirrors your environmental concern. Become part of the decision-making process if you want to have a really effective say.

PEOPLE POWER

Never underestimate people power. A great example of this is the boycott American housewives placed on a multinational company which marketed and sold powdered milk to mothers of young babies in Third World countries. Because badly polluted water was all the mothers had to mix with the powdered milk, thousands of infants were dying. A few American housewives took up the cause and advocated a boycott on all the company's products. The American public backed them up and the seven-year boycott cost the company millions of dollars.

Another positive step you can take is to join a major conservation group. Their effectiveness is often dictated by their membership – political parties can't ignore organisations that have thousands of members. Larger groups usually circulate regular newletters to keep members informed.

INDEX